Praise for

"The most important book I have read. I study it like a bible!" Elisabeth Kubler-Ross, M.D.

"These words embody tolerance, universality, love and compassion—hallmarks of all Great Teachings. They turn our attention inward to our own divine nature, instead of diverting it outward. Paul Ferrini is a modern-day Kahlil Gibran—poet, mystic, visionary, teller of truth." Larry Dossey, M.D.

"Paul Ferrini leads us skillfully and courageously beyond shame, blame and attachment to our wounds into the depths of self-forgiveness. His work is a must-read for all people who are ready to take responsibility for their own healing." John Bradshaw.

"A breath of fresh air in an often musty and cluttered domain. With sweetness, clarity, and simplicity we are directed to the truth within. I read this book whenever my heart directs, which is often." Pat Rodegast.

"Paul Ferrini's writing is authentic, delightful and wise. It reconnects the reader to the Spirit Within, to that place where even our deepest wounds can be healed." Joan Borysenko, Ph.D.

"I feel that this work comes from a continuous friendship with the deepest part of the Self. I trust its wisdom." Coleman Barks, poet and translator.

"Paul Ferrini's wonderful books show a way to walk lightly with joy on planet earth." Gerald Jampolsky, M.D.

"Paul Ferrini leads us on a gentle journey to our true source of joy and happiness—inside ourselves." Ken Keyes, Jr.

Book Design by Paul Ferrini
Layout by Aryeh Swisa

ISBN # 1-879159-35-X

Manufactured in the United States of America

Return to the GARDEN

Reflections of the Christ Mind - Part IV

PAUL FERRINI

Table of Contents

Part One: The Encounter

Part Two: The Teaching

Part Three: The Practice

Part One
The Encounter

Hearing The Voice

Born into an Atheist family, I had little use for religion or spirituality until I was twenty three years old. I was living then in East Cambridge, Massachusetts. I had just completed graduate school and had been searching in vain for a teaching position. Needing to put bread on the table, I took a job driving a truck.

Each day I got up at 4:00 AM and rode my bicycle to work through the cold, windy streets of Cambridge, loaded up my truck and began my deliveries in downtown Boston. As I drove over the bridge by the Museum of Science, the pale muted rays of dawn struggled to penetrate the clouds. It felt gruesome to me.

Light was having a hard time making it into the darkness of this world. When I looked around me, all I saw was exploitation and suffering. When I looked within, all I felt was sadness and pain. I saw no reason for being here.

My life was solitary. I had ended a long-term relationship earlier that year. I was in mourning for that connection and unable to reach out to others. I had not been able to find work in my chosen field. And I had just moved from the quiet and beauty of Vermont back to the city. I was having trouble adjusting to the noises of police and fire sirens screeching in the middle of the night. I could not understand the gangs of kids that roamed the streets at 3 AM throwing barrels full of trash out onto Cambridge Street.

Everyone in the city seemed angry or sad. I wasn't much different, except that I lived for the poems I wrote when I got home from work. They supplied the only meaning in my life. If my life did not shift somehow by the time I completed the collection of poems I was writing, there would be no reason to continue it.

I was depressed, suicidal. When I drove across the bridge into Boston, dawn continued to announce to me its anguish. I appropriately entitled my collection of poems "The Thorns of Dawn."

I did not know at the time that I was experiencing my own crucifixion. I did not know that life was bringing me to the edge of death so that I could be reborn in Spirit. I did not know that I had to experience the utter meaninglessness of life to recover its original meaning.

When I finished that collection of poems, I talked to God for the second time in my life. I talked to God, even though I doubted His existence. Even though He had refused to answer me at age thirteen when my cousin Deirdre had died of Leukemia. Reeling in deep existential pain since that day of lost innocence, I could never reconcile the idea of God with the seemingly needless suffering I saw around me. "Give me one reason why I should not abandon this meaningless world?" I asked, sitting at the kitchen table. I was not expecting an answer.

"Go into the Living Room, close your eyes and take the first book you come to in the bookcase," I heard a very clear, firm voice say in my mind.

"What do I have to lose?" I thought, getting up and walking into the living room. I closed my eyes, put my hands out and let them move toward the bookshelf. I pulled out a single book and opened my eyes. It was *I and Thou* by Martin Buber.

I opened the book to the first page and began reading. After the first paragraph or two, it became clear that I had my answer. I sank down into the book, hearing each word spoken into my ears, drinking the truth with a profound thirst I did not know I had.

I wanted an answer and I got one. Life was not just the shell of sadness I was seeing. It was more.

"There are two worlds," Buber told me, "the world of I-It and the World of I-Thou." The world of I-It I knew only too well. It was the world of exploitation, struggle, greed, selfishness, layers upon layers of suffering. That was the world I wanted to escape.

But there was also another world, Buber maintained. It was the world of union, relationship, trust, and grace. It was the world of unconditional acceptance and love. Even though I had experienced only brief glimpses of this world of "I-Thou," I knew of its existence.

I had to admit the fact that the world was not all suffering. It was perhaps 99% suffering, and 1% grace. Was I willing to stick around for that 1% chance of unconditional love? I didn't think so.

But then the voice in the book spoke into my opening heart and said: "It's up to you which world you want to see!"

With just a single sentence, my self-pitying, state of-the-world-bemoaning attitude was stripped of its artifice. Now the emperor had no clothes. Suffering was not a dictum, but a choice. It was up to me which world I chose to see.

You mean I could choose to see grace all of the time? You mean the quality of my experience did not depend on what was outside of me, but on the attitude I brought to it? You mean the "I" in "I-Thou" was my responsibility, not somebody else's, not even God's?

I reeled from the words even as they resonated like waves inside of me. I knew they were truth, but letting them in would change my entire life. Never again would I be able to play the role of victim or innocent bystander.

If the world I inhabited depended on how I saw it and stood in relationship to it, then I had homework for the rest of my embodiment. I had to stop looking outside at what others were doing, and begin looking inside, at the contents of my own consciousness.

I was responsible for whether my "I" was the "I" in the relational event "I-Thou" or the "I" in the non-relational, manipulative event "I-It." Every moment I made a choice for joy or sadness, love or fear. My dialogue with God depended on which "I" approached Him/Her. If I approached as "I-It", S/he could not hear me or answer me, because S/he did not live there.

That explained the stony silence I encountered at age thirteen when I begged God to give back Deirdre and take me instead. At that time, I came to God not as the lover comes to the beloved, but as the victim comes to the executioner to beg a few crumbs. I did not come for understanding to a God of love, one who cared for me and for Deirdre too. Instead I came to a God of fear, who capriciously gives and takes away. I came to the Grim Reaper with a grisly proposition fitting only for such a Being: "Take me, you cruel, bloodthirsty Ogre and give Deirdre back instead."

At thirteen the "I" that came to God was the "I" in the non-relational event "I-It." At twenty-three the "I" addressed by the powerful, resonant voice within was the "I" in the relational event "I-Thou." The Beloved was calling. How could the Lover not respond?

When we feel unworthy, it is hard to believe that we are the one chosen by God to bring love into this world. Yet every despairing man or woman who gets on his or her knees and asks for help is a chosen one.

By repudiating the world of suffering, we ask for a better way. And asking, we are not only given the way, but asked to walk it, asked to bring the light we find in the darkness of our own hearts to others who are calling out for it. Our God works in strange and magnificent ways, always lifting us up, always giving the gift through our hands.

We are the ones who must learn to bring affection to the loved-starved children of our hearts and minds. If we don't bring it, who else will bring it? And If we can bring it to ourselves, then we can also bring it to all of the sons and daughters of God who do not know that they are loved and cherished just the way they are.

In my living room, I was given my homework for the rest of my incarnation. I was not here on this earth to be a victim of a callous, uncaring world. I was here to give birth to love in my own heart and to carry that love to everyone in my experience. I was not the victim or the executioner, but the king offering the stay of sentence. I was the savior, pointing the way of redemption. I did not know it then, but Christ had taken hold of me and wherever I walked from that day on, he walked with me hand in hand.

Seeking and Finding

My life from that day forward was not particularly eventful. I read many books by Martin Buber. I devoured the words of the Baal Shem Tov, Rabbi Nachman, and the great Hasidic Rabbis. I discovered a joyful and soulful vein of love teaching within the core of Judaism which enabled me to embrace the Jewish side of my heritage.

But I also found myself seeking God through my mind. I became thirsty for knowledge. I studied the

Cabbalah, the Egyptian Tarot, esoteric astrology and psychology. I studied Buddhist, Hindu and Taoist Scriptures, humanistic, transpersonal and Jungian psychology. I developed my intuition and used both left brain and right brain approaches to understanding human behavior. I did charts and readings and counseling sessions.

My clients were happy, but I wasn't. It seemed that the more I learned the further I got from the truth. I began to realize that I had become preoccupied with my tools. There was no joy in them. The intellect, try as hard as it could, would never be able to fathom the meaning of human experience or the way in which the divine intersected it.

It was at this time that I picked up *A Course in Miracles*, a book written by Helen Schuckman, a research psychologist at Columbia University in New York. This book claimed to be written by Jesus through Helen.

When I picked the book up, I had the same experience I had when I read *I and Thou*. I heard the words spoken in my ear and felt them resonate like waves throughout my body. I knew this teaching was the next step on my spiritual path, that it came from the same source as the previous material.

But I felt very uncomfortable with the idea that

18

Jesus wrote the material and I didn't like the Christian terminology or the archaic style of prose the book was written in. Why would a book which I knew intuitively to be the truth come in a form which was so distasteful to me? Why did we need 1100 pages to express the truth when Lao Tzu needed only 81?

It took several years for me to realize that only *A Course in Miracles* could have brought me to Jesus. I may not have liked how it was written, but I did like what it said. It was the real teaching of Jesus, the one I knew in my heart. It had psychological depth and intellectual consistency. It could stand up alongside the most sophisticated teachings of the East.

It spoke to my skeptical side. And even though I had a little trouble at first using terms like "Holy Spirit," I knew that I could substitute the word "Tao" without changing the meaning. Holy Spirit was still the impersonal God energy that manifests equally through each one of us, just as the Tao does.

The most important aspect of this material was its focus on our own relationship to the divine and its contention that each one of us could have an ongoing relationship with God in our hearts and minds. We could ask for help and receive it. We could bring our problems to God and S/he would guide us how to proceed in a way that would honor everyone in our experience. *A Course in Miracles* was not just a theology, but a practical method for living in the consciousness of God.

Unfortunately, the majority of the people I met who were working with the *Course* were trying to understand it or teach it. They weren't letting the material come into their hearts and their lives. They weren't practicing it. And without practice, this was yet another system of knowledge that points at the truth. To take the truth in, practice is necessary.

During this period, I began working with the material in a heart-centered, experiential way. I invited people to conferences and workshops where they could practice the material. I published a magazine encouraging diversity and open discussion, and discouraging dogmatic approaches. I wanted our community to walk its talk, to be the embodiment of love in action.

Then, I began hearing a voice within that said "I want you to acknowledge me." Whenever I would teach, the voice would remind me, but I ignored it. There was only one person I was not acknowledging and I didn't want to acknowledge him. I didn't want to get up and say "Jesus is my teacher." I didn't want to say "Jesus is the author of *A Course in Miracles*."

But the more I resisted, the louder the voice got. I began having dreams in which Jesus would speak to me. These dreams were surrealistic and strangely life-like. In one dream I was in a large cave. There were several figures dressed in brown hooded robes. Out of the corner of my eye, I saw one of them bend down to pick up a gleaming broadsword. Then he turned, carrying the sword in front of his heart, and walked directly toward me. As he came close, I looked into his face, and I knew that this was Jesus. We looked deeply into each other's eyes, and then he placed the sword flat against my heart. I felt unbelievable energy go through my body. I was cat-apulted back against the stone wall and fell to the ground. Jesus came to where I was lying and looked down at me. "You see," he said. "This energy is real and you will use it to heal as I did."

He made a gesture toward his third eye and said "You must have the absolute conviction of the inno-cence of the other person here and," pointing to his heart "unconditional love and acceptance for the person here. Then, these mental and emotional energies triangulate with the hands, so that healing flows through the hands to the other person. If that person can receive the truth that you are thinking and the love that you are feeling, then they can also receive the extension of that truth and that love, which is flowing through your hands.

Later, in the dream, Jesus answered several of my questions. In particular, I asked him about sections of *A Course in Miracles,* in which he supposedly claimed that our physical bodies and the world that we live in were actually creations of our ego structure.

"It is true," he said, "neither the body nor the world are ultimate reality, but they are not to be denied or denigrated either. "Everything can be lifted up through the power of unconditional love."

The body could be a vehicle through which love expresses. The world could be a place where love and compassion make their home. To say that they are created by the ego is to miss the point. It is how they are used that matters.

Are they used by ego or by the true Self? Buber had taught me earlier, the "I" in "I-It" was not the same "I" as the "I" in "I-Thou." The body used in a loving way was not the same as the body used in an angry or fearful way. The problem was not "the body" or "the world." It was what we put into them.

Sex, for example, is neither good nor bad. If there is love in it, then sexuality becomes an expression of that love. If there is no love in it, then sex becomes empty and unfulfilling.

"Everything can be lifted up," he told me, "by the power of unconditional love." It is not what you do so much as how you do it.

Jesus is teacher of love. He does not want to tell us what to do in every situation. He does not favor 613 commandments, such as we have in the Talmud. Even ten commandments are probably more than we can handle. He gives us just two: "Love your neighbor as yourself" and "put no other Gods before Him."

Let God come first in your life and love your neighbor. A very simple teaching, but a very challenging practice.

As I began to feel the energy of Jesus come into my life, I experienced a deep kinship toward him and his teaching. It was so simple, so pure.

Clearly, we had lost sight of the pure teaching. What we had was not what he gave us, but what others gave us in his name.

What was clear to me in reading *A Course in Miracles* and what was viscerally clear now that I was in dialogue with him was that the fear and guilt-based teachings of the church had nothing to do with Jesus.

Anyone who knows Jesus in his or her heart knows this as an inner certainty. Jesus is an uncompromising teacher of love. His ferocity comes from his commitment to love and his insistence that love is the only answer to our problems.

Not only was Jesus' teaching constantly in my mind, but I felt his presence in and around me. Shortly after I had the cave dream, hands-on healers began to come into my life. At the time, I was putting on large conferences for students of *A Course in Miracles* and I invited many of these healers to come to these events as speakers and workshop leaders. This pushed the buttons of *Course* purists who had adopted an anti-body attitude.

At one conference, there were a number of healings that took place. In fact, during the whole conference I could feel Jesus' presence behind me. Energy would be pouring though my heart. And, whenever I hugged anyone, I could feel that there was a transmission of energy through my heart and hands.

My heart was on fire. My body was burning up. I didn't think I could stand it. I was riding in a cocoon of energy. It felt so delicious, I didn't want to come out of it, yet so intense I wondered if I could stay in it without exploding.

People would come to these conferences, experience this energy, and then go home and crash. That didn't feel right to me. I knew that we had to give people a way to feel connected to the Christ energy when they got home. So we began to develop the *Affinity Group Process.* Jesus concurred. "The time for these large conferences will soon pass, he said. "Before long, you will be working more deeply with smaller groups."

At our conferences, people would be able to feel the Christ energy, but they didn't know where it came from or how they could stay connected to it. Where it came from was very simple. When people were willing to put their judgments aside and live from a place of trust, they would go into ecstasy. They would look into the eyes of total strangers and fall in love. They could feel this kind of love, not just for a few people, but for everyone. It was the kind of love that happened when you let yourself fall into the heart. Anyone standing before you would receive that love, because as long as you stayed in your heart, you could not stop giving it.

But as soon as the judgments came back and were entertained, as soon as fear came up and got a foothold, then the defensive shield would come down over the heart and the flow of love in and out would stop. You could see this happen for individuals. Someone would push their buttons and they would retreat to their rooms. Then, the fear and judgment would pass, and they would come back to the group to recharge.

People didn't realize that the experience of ecstasy originated inside themselves, in the dropping of their judgments and expectations. They did not know that their ability to become an open channel through which love flowed unimpeded depended on their own internal surrender. So they were not able to carry this experience home.

They kept coming back to the conferences to "fill up" their empty tanks with love. But that love would always be short-lived because it was not fueled by their own surrender.

As we began to shift the responsibility from the presenters and entertainers to each participant, the conferences got smaller and smaller. "You are the only subject of this gathering," we told people. "Nobody else has the answers for you. Your connection to love is an internal proposition, not an external one." As we integrated the *Affinity Process* more and more into our gatherings, people began to get it. They began to realize the they were the light and the love of the world. They were the vehicle through which wisdom and love could express. Not just one or two of them. But every one of them. Christ was not just something experienced by Jesus. It was in all of us.

The Master Teacher

It was always amazing to me that students of *A Course in Miracles* could believe that Jesus spoke through Helen, yet doubt that he could speak through others. As I began to acknowledge and surrender to my own connection to Jesus, I realized that he spoke to so many people in different ways. I recognized his energy and guidance behind the Twelve Steps of Alcoholics Anonymous. I heard him speak through "born again" Christians. I saw his presence in the simple acts of caring and service done by hundreds of individuals with no religion to preach nor any axe to grind.

Anyone embodying unconditional love, acceptance and forgiveness was his messenger, his disciple. Some knew it. Some did not. But that was not important. What was important was that, through them, love was offered. And having given love, they could not help but receive it. The more they gave, the more they received. There was no deficiency of love in the world. Love lived in the heart of every human being. As it was trusted and expressed, love became present in the world. Through this process, everyone and everything would "be lifted up."

In my conversations with him, Jesus has never claimed to be the only son of God. He has never claimed to have died for our sins, to have walked on water, to have been born of a virgin or to have physically resurrected his body. Instead, he maintains that we are all sons and daughters of God, that we can all die to our sins and reclaim our innocence. Just as he was, we too are crucified by our egoic experience, and we too can be uplifted by the power of love to realize our true nature even while we are here in this body in this world.

Jesus has always told me "What I can do you too can do, if you are willing." He has always considered himself to be an equal. When I have sought to raise him up, he has lowered himself down to look me squarely in the eyes. And whenever I have tried to raise myself up above any of my brothers or sisters, he has told me: "lest you love the least of them, you do not love me."

Jesus does not speak for one man or woman, but for all human beings. He holds each one of us dear, and refuses to let anyone think s/he is better or worse, higher or lower than the next. In Jesus' eyes we are all equally spiritual. The Pope is no holier than the prostitute or drunk on the street. Clearly, we have many biases and opinions to surrender if we would see each other as Jesus sees us.

While Jesus does not suggest that this body or this earth represents ultimate reality, he would have us treat the body and the earth with respect. In respecting the forms in and through which we live, we also respect the breath that gives life to them and uplifts them.

Love itself is ultimate reality. It is the beginning and the end, the alpha and the omega. It is the original creative spark, its fullness, and its self- containment. It emanates from itself, expresses itself and rests in itself. Whether rising or falling, waxing or waning, ebbing or flowing, it never loses touch with what it is. In the same manner, when we are in communion with love, we never lose touch with who we are.

While we live in this body and this world, we can commune with ultimate reality. We can experience love, giving it and receiving it. We can also get attached to this body and this world and close down our connection with ultimate reality. When that happens we experience pain. We suffer.

This wakes us up. It helps us remember that we cannot be happy unless we are in communion with love. Fortunately, we are never more than one thought away from love. When we lose touch with love, we have only to think a loving thought and love comes flowing into our hearts.

Death may dissolve the body and the world, but it cannot dissolve love, because love is eternal. It is not dependent on a particular body or personality.

Jesus may not be present here in a body, but he is present in the love. When we tune into the love, we tune into Jesus. It is that simple.

If you are looking for Jesus, the historical figure, it may be hard for you to find him. That body/mind construct ceased to be ages ago. But if you are looking for Jesus, the loving contemporary presence, then you do not have very far to look. Whenever you speak to him, he is there. You just need to be quiet to hear his voice. You just need to be still to feel his presence next to you.

Having a personal relationship with Jesus is the essence of Christianity. Unless you feel the presence of Jesus, unless you hear and follow his guidance right here and right now, it will be difficult for you to follow his teaching.

Jesus is not some abstract image from the past, but a living reality. He is not in a separate body but he lives in the love that uplifts all bodies, all hearts and all minds. You can think with him, feel with him, breathe with him.

The compassionate presence that gave us the teaching of love and forgiveness two thousand years ago is still giving it to us now. The voice of God is still speaking to us, through Jesus and other great beings who have joined with him in this great work of At-One-ment.

Every time one person wakes up to the truth about himself or herself, a great sun rises in the heart of the archetypal human, radiating its light and its love to all of us. No wonder we feel his love. No wonder we feel the love of all beings who have our greatest good at heart.

The Divine In The Human

The life of Jesus is a metaphor for the highest spiritual teaching. As such, it retains all the power of Myth. We believe that Jesus had a divine origin, that he was sent by God to redeem us. To highlight his divine origin, we have the story of the virgin birth. We believe that Jesus did not come from the human milieu, that he was not conceived by a sexual act, but was a divine gift given to Mary as acknowledgement of her chastity and her faith.

If we believe that this divine origin was true only for Jesus or perhaps Mary too, then we set them apart from us. We put them on a pedestal. They are divine and we are human. They are the beloved of God and we are mere sinners. Needless to say, this is not a teaching of empowerment.

If you look at the life of Jesus, you will see that he never placed himself above others. He sought out the poor, the ill, the disenfranchised. He kept company with lepers and prostitutes. He carried the teaching wherever he went. His was not a gospel for the rich and famous or the spiritual elite. It was a gospel for every man and woman. It empowered even the lowest of the low with dignity and respect.

Jesus did not attempt to put himself on a pedestal. He sought to raise everyone up. If he was of divine origin, then so were we. Whatever he could do, we could do and more. He did not want special status. He wanted to show us the way that we too could walk. He led not just by words, but also by example.

If we want a personal relationship with Jesus, it must be with the man, not with the Myth. He fit the archetype of the Godman, the divine in the human. As such he is larger than life. How can one have a relationship with the only Son of God? Surely, this is as difficult as having a relationship with God Himself.

Any such relationship is bound to be special, privileged. Of course, specialness and privilege were part of the conceit of the Jewish tradition. Were they not "the chosen people?"

Did Jesus come to continue the tradition of specialness or to destroy it once and for all? Did he come to remind us of our equality with each other and our inner connection with God or did he come to create yet another spiritual elite? Was he a teacher of universal truth or parochial dispensation?

In truth, his teaching was the most radical to come to the planet. "Love everyone, even your enemies...turn the other cheek...judge not lest you also be judged." He was not milktoast, but the fire in the oven.

He came to create a revolution within Judaism, to turn it away from narrow parochialism and specialness, to open it into a universal teaching available to all. He did not come to create another narrow religion.

Were he here today in body, Jesus would be neither a Jew nor a Christian. He would live and teach beyond labels, beyond prejudice, beyond ideas that separate one person from another. Were he here today, his teaching would threaten those in positions of power and privilege just as it did in his day. And it is likely that he would be plotted against, betrayed, and handed over to the very authorities he threatens. Perhaps he would not be crucified, but he might spend his life in prison or perhaps await a more clinical execution on death row.

So long as we deny the potential of our own Christhood, we will continue to crucify the Christ outside of us. That is why Jesus is not here in body today. He does not need a repeat performance of the passion play, nor do we.

We need to realize that where Jesus once walked so do we. The passion play is not his now, but ours. We need to decide whether we want to continue to carry our cross up the hill, or put it down. If we insist on carrying it, we will not be the only ones to be crucified. Others will follow dutifully in our footsteps.

But if we lay our cross down, those who follow us can be spared their journey of fear and guilt and a new day can dawn on earth, a day when the Christ is celebrated in each one of us, rather than crucified upon a cross. That day is coming. And Jesus is doing everything he can to help us bring it. If we will listen to him and practice his teaching, if we will model it in the world by embodying love and compassion, then it will not be long. We are his footsoldiers. Now that we have put down our burden of guilt and fear, our load is lighter and we can work more lovingly and confidently.

The journey to the cross, the crucifixion, and the resurrection is not history, but Myth. Just as Jesus returns to his divine home unscathed by the brutality of the world, so do we. Although it seems that our journey here is filled with pain and suffering, there is part of us that remains untouched, as innocent as a babe wrapped in swaddling clothes. Like Jesus, we too are resurrected. Not because we are perfect. Not because we are mistake free, but because we have learned to forgive our mistakes and those of others.

By loving and accepting our humanness as Jesus did, we begin to connect to the essence of love, our divine origin. We meet the essential Self who was not born and will not die, the Self which cannot be hurt or compromised, even though this passion play might lead us to believe otherwise.

The key to our redemption depends in large extent on our ability to hold our shadowy side with compassion. The Son of God does not deny the presence of fear or project it onto someone else. He lets the fear come up and be held by love. Because it is held by love, the fear dissolves.

By emphasizing love, all that is not love surrenders in the awareness that love is what it wants. Jesus has told us many times "Resist not evil." To resist the dark side merely empowers it.

If we stuff our fears, we become terrified that they will re-appear when we least expect them. If we project them, we spend our lives defending ourselves against imagined attack. Fear cannot be repressed or projected without being strengthened. Jesus knew that.

When the fear is welcomed by love, it is transformed. Lack cannot exist in the face of abundant supply. How can fear sustain itself if it feels the presence of love?

Accepting our humanness is the way to the divine presence within. For the human was made in the divine image. There is nothing bad about it. There is nothing bad about our fear or anyone else's. Our fears simply need to rest inside the love they are seeking. Otherwise, we go about seeking love through our fear. And that doesn't work. When fear seeks love, it only finds itself.

Inside the man Jesus is the Christ. When Jesus is okay with Jesus, including all his pain and all his fear, he becomes the Christ. It is no different for us. When we have accepted all the aspects of self of which we were once ashamed, when we are holding our fears and those of others compassionately, we too become the Christ.

A true Christian does not worship Jesus and place him on a pedestal. S/he internalizes his teaching and becomes the Christ.

In the Jewish tradition, the Messiah cannot come as long as one man or woman attempts to live outside the embrace of love. Jesus brought us the teaching that will enable all of us to return to the arms of love. We have only to practice that teaching.

In that sense, the decision each one of us makes is crucial. For the Messiah does not come from on high. S/he comes in the hearts of each one of us.

Return To The Garden

In the beginning, we lived in blind obedience to the law. We did what we were told and we were rewarded appropriately. We were God's beloved, but we had never tasted freedom. We were happy to be cherished by God, but we wanted more. We wanted freedom.

Like Prometheus, we had to steel the fire of the gods. We had no choice. To evolve, we had to learn to become love-givers, not just love-receivers.

We all know what happened then. We were cast out of the Garden and for the first time in our lives we felt shame. We hid ourselves from God and from each other.

Before we plucked fruit from trees that grew all year long. They knew no winter, spring, or fall, but perpetual summer, nor did we know struggle or hardship. All our needs were provided for.

When we left the garden, we faced the task of providing for ourselves. We needed to know what to think and what to do. We had become responsible for our own lives. We had to make choices.

The price of free will was high indeed. But it was freedom we wanted.

Unconscious happiness was not enough. We wanted to become conscious. We wanted to wake up. We did not know that waking up would mean making lots of mistakes and judging ourselves and others mercilessly for those errors. We did not know that self-crucifixion would become a way of life.

From the garden of grace to the garden of Gethsemane, from unconscious bliss to conscious shame, we moved until the fall was complete. And there we stood grounded, shivering in the cold, without faith in ourselves, unable even to turn to God.

Slowly and painfully, we learned to have faith in ourselves. We cut down trees, tilled the soil, planted seeds, and brought in the harvest. We labored from dawn until dusk. We built roads and railroads, great cities and industrial centers. We extended our civilization out into the prairies and mountains, to the edge of the sea. We survived drought and pestilence, floods, fires, and hurricanes. We triumphed over the earth. We subdued the animals of the field and the birds of the air. In our eyes, we earned the dominion once promised to us.

But along the way, we made mistakes. We became restless, irresponsible, greedy. We polluted our rivers and streams. We burned our own cities. Our jails filled to overflowing. Murders, rapists, and child molesters walked our streets. The earth groaned under the onslaught of endless roads, landfills and construction sites. Plutonium was buried deep in the heart of the earth. Oil spills stained the pristine waters of far-off shorelines and birds lay lifeless on the beach. Even the sky was torn open, leaving huge gaps in the ozone layer.

We began to realize that our version of the Garden was not as good as God's. Prophets began to ring the bells of doom and gloom. Earthchanges were coming. God was angry at us and we were going to have to pay for our sins. As the millennium approached, judgment day seemed to be coming with it.

So we began to talk to God again. Hundreds of thousands of people began calling out. Even Atheists and agnostics began to pray. We all needed to know where we stood. Was this hysteria just millennium fever, or was Armageddon on its way?

When I asked my teacher, he said: "To return to the garden, you must move to the other side of your fear. You cannot pretend not to be afraid, nor can you be ruled by your fears. You must learn to hold those fears in the most profound silence. Only when you come to the end of the proliferating mind stuff, can you face the next moment in a loving way."

"Beware of false prophets," he had told us before. "It is true that you must learn to be responsible for your actions. But the laws of the earth are not vindictive. They don't seek to punish you. You can understand them and work with them. Indeed, now is the time to understand and cooperate. The earth is talking to you. It is time to listen to her.

God's Mouthpiece

I once received a letter from a woman who told me that she had been very moved by these Christ Mind materials, but because of her upbringing she needed to understand how I could speak for Jesus.

Many others have had similar questions. They have wondered why I don't call what I do channeling. Am I not bringing the words and presence of Jesus through?

The truth is that Jesus came into my life. I did not ask for a relationship with him, at least consciously. I simply experienced a profound resonance with this teaching. I heard the words of *A Course in Miracles* spoken into my ears, as were the teachings of Martin Buber. The *Course* seemed to be a direct extension of Buber's earlier teachings about relationship. In my heart, I knew I was being called into this work. On some inner level, I knew and understood it. It was in every cell of my body. Without knowing why, I had the complete conviction of its truth.

My ego was not too happy with this direction. I didn't have much respect for Christianity, so it was hard to open to Jesus. I had to let him speak to me directly. I had to accept his inner authority. I had to realize that all of the injustices perpetrated by the Christian church had nothing to do with Jesus, his energy or his teachings.

I simply became willing to listen to him. I opened to a relationship which brought me not only clear understanding, but boundless acceptance and love. I knew in my heart of hearts that my purpose in this embodiment was to embrace these teachings fully and to be a mouthpiece for them.

Early on, Jesus made it clear to me that my job was just to show up and he would do the rest. In the beginning of this work, I was self-conscious. When I gave a talk or a workshop, I tried to prepare for it, make notes, think it through. One day, I kept hearing this voice inside that said "No Notes. Your job is just to show up." I tried to ignore it. I went back to my room and began writing notes about the material I expected to cover in my workshop the next morning. I was quite pleased with myself and went to bed feeling prepared. The next morning I woke up and read over my notes. I was amazed. They were utter gibberish!

I went to my workshop with my mind totally blank. I kept hearing the words "Just show up. It will be fine." And so I went to my workshop and even when I opened my mouth to speak, I did not know what words would come out. As I needed them, each word and sentence came into my consciousness and I spoke them.

After the workshop, people came up to me and thanked me enthusiastically. I felt strangely detached. I didn't feel that I had done anything. And I hadn't.

I hadn't given the workshop, but who had? Well, I suppose it could have been Holy Spirit or my Inner Guidance that did it. In fact, it would have been much easier for me to think "it's just the impersonal Spirit of God coming through me." But the instructions "No notes. Just show up and I'll do the rest" came in the context of an inner dialog in which Jesus was asking me to acknowledge him as my teacher.

Increasingly, he made it clear to me that my ego was to step aside when I spoke or taught. The way I could do that was by just showing up and having no idea what was about to happen. By surrendering to the moment, I could meet it with open arms.

In truth, he was training me to do what he had learned to do: to surrender the part of the mind that wants to be in control so that I could rely on God within. He was there as a kind of gatekeeper, helping me open the door to the divine presence within.

Jesus was not separate from that presence, nor was I. In fact, you might say that as I trusted and walked through the door, I joined Jesus there, in the eternal embrace of God communion. To join him, I had to surrender to the Christ within me. Once I became one with the Christ within me, I was not separate from him or from God.

As I have learned to trust more and more — often

43

getting up in front of over a thousand people without any idea of what I would say — I began to realize that all I was doing in my work was opening the same door that Jesus held open for me. I was helping people set their judgments aside and enter into a state of love communion in which they too became the Christ. When the words that came out of my mouth resonated deeply in the hearts and minds of my listeners, they would open to the truth within their own experience. Only the Christ within them could hear and experience the Christ within me.

So what is the authority that enables me to speak the words of the teaching that I know in my heart comes from Jesus? It is not an outer authority, but an inner one. It is the same authority that enabled Jesus to say "I and the Father are One." It is the same authority Moses claimed when he brought down the tablets of the law.

All prophets are attuned to the voice of God. And that voice is not outside of them, but within their consciousness, in their heart of hearts. You might not believe it, but that voice is in your heart too.

Jesus belongs to the prophetic tradition. I may have come to it kicking and screaming, but it is my tradition too. It is the path to God that begins with the rejection of idols. It is the path that asks us to turn to the mystery within.

If you feel the resonance of these words, it is probably your path too. It doesn't matter if you are Christian or Jewish or Muslim. It is one tradition, not two, or three. Even if you have never believed in God, if you are willing to trust and look within for guidance, you can be sure that the path will open to you too.

As it applies to this tradition, the question "By whose authority do you speak or act?" can only be answered: "By the authority of the God Within."   If you ask Moses or Jesus or Mohammed, this is what they will tell you. And they are the wayshowers, are they not? Would they then expect us to give a different answer?

I speak to you therefore not as someone who has a special relationship with Jesus or with God, but as someone who has discovered the Christ within. And in that discovery, I am one with my teacher, Jesus of Nazareth. You can be one with him too, if you open your heart to his teaching and his presence in your life.

The word channeling as it is commonly used cannot do justice to the relationship event we speak of. Therefore I prefer not to use it. But I recognize the truth that we are all potential prophets or channels for truth in that we are capable of stepping aside and letting the voice of God (in whatever form we hear it) speak to us and through us.

The Renewal of the Covenant

In every generation, the truth must be encountered directly by prophets, mystics and visionaries. Becoming one with that truth, they can express it in the language of their times.

When prophets, mystics and visionaries express the truth, they often challenge the institutions, dominant beliefs, and the authority figures of their society. That is what Jesus did.

These people claim an inner authority, not an outer one. They oppose and expose all forms of hypocrisy and injustice, even when it is institutionalized. As such, they are not very popular with the powers that be.

Because they seek to empower people to think for themselves and take responsibility for their lives, the teachings of the prophets, mystics and visionaries often ignite the hearts of people. They encourage people to ask questions, to challenge old customs and laws that no longer serve the greatest good.

Their impact is awakening within the consciousness of individuals and revolutionary within the collective consciousness.

Through the authentic life and teaching of such individuals, truth remains a living force. It is modeled in their actions. Through their humor, their compassion, their courage, we see spirit at work in the world.

In contrast to the prophets, the mystics, and the visionaries, there are the fundamentalists: people who like to live their lives based on a past authority. They look at the Bible or some other holy book as literally true. They are concerned about the letter of the law, not the spirit of it. When Jesus was born, the Pharisees were the fundamentalists, but fundamentalists can be found within every religious tradition. Now, we have fundamentalist Christians and Muslims too.

Fundamentalists tend to feel that there is only one truth and they alone have it. They are often intolerant of other paths and work hard to convert others to their beliefs. They often profess their beliefs with great zeal, but this zeal in itself seems to hide an inner insecurity. Were they secure about their own relationship with God, they would not be threatened by others who held different values and beliefs.

In every generation, fundamentalism opposes the rediscovery of truth within the hearts and minds of human beings. It emphasizes an outer authority, rather than an inner one. It establishes spiritual hierarchies and creates new idols. It substitutes elaborate rules and rituals for the authentic practice of God-communion and sacrifices the freedom of the individual to the tyranny of the group mind.

It is into this narrowing focus of consciousness that Christ is born today, as he was two thousand years ago. And as S/he is realized in the hearts and minds of people today, the prophetic tradition is renewed. New scriptures are received and brought through by mystics and visionaries. The eternal truth is understood in the context of the time in which we live.

In some respects, this is a confusing time to be on the planet. Today, there are hundreds of thousands of books, tapes, lectures, and workshops claiming to point the way toward truth. Every path you can imagine is being offered, from angel guidance to satanic rituals, from the witchcraft to the new physics, indeed from the ridiculous to the sublime. It is hard for some people to discriminate.

The old, hierarchical religion is in its death throws. The patriarchal God of retribution is done in. There are no more chosen people. Now, every one of us is chosen.

We can no longer take our direction from churches or gurus. We must find it in our own hearts. We must try new ideas and experiment with new practices, learning what works and what does not. We must learn to discriminate. We must take responsibility for our own path and learn to honor the path of others.

It is an exciting time. It puts the responsibility squarely on us.

Will we make mistakes?   Absolutely.

Will we try some ideas that don't work, perhaps hurting ourselves in the process. Very likely.

But we will learn from all this and move on.

We will struggle with layers and layers of shame and guilt until we come face to face with our own innocence. And when we do, we will fall back into the heart, and realize that nothing we have ever thought, said or done can ultimately condemn us. Because right now, we have a choice. And right now, we choose to be gentle with ourselves and each other.

Compassion is not born over night, nor is responsibility. But you can be sure that both are being born in us right now.

Where is the Garden?

When we ate from the tree of knowledge, we chose to become conscious of how life works. We entered into a path of mistake-making and correction which would bring us true knowledge of self and other.

Before we ate the fruit of that tree, we lived in blind trust and faith. God's grace flowed to us automatically. We did not have to do anything to deserve it. We were loved, but we did not know why.

We wanted to know. We wanted to participate in the drama of creation, to know what our creator knew, to learn to create like Him. That desire led to our birth into form.

To know creation, we had to become it. Thus began our self-imposed exile from God's everpresent love and grace.

It was a choice made with great courage. We gave up the comfort of absolute truth for the discomfort of relative knowledge. From that moment, we would strive for the absolute, but encounter only the relative. The path of knowledge did not seem to lead back to God. Indeed, it often seemed to take us away from It.

We acted with great courage. Yet God had even

greater courage. He released us on our quest for knowledge knowing full well we would walk through the land of darkness, encountering dragons and demons. He knew we would get caught in the dynamics of blame and shame, punishing ourselves and each other. He knew we would come to the brink of destroying ourselves, yet he still let us go. He had the courage to observe our suffering, indeed even feel it, without intervening in the choice we had made.

Perhaps he knew something we also knew when we left the garden, but now have difficulty remembering. He knew that his spark, his seed, his love and his truth, was living within us. He knew that as soon as we learned to turn to that love, we would begin to embody it. And so the covenant between Him and us would be renewed. We would find light in the darkness. Not just His light, but our own as well. That light and that love were our inheritance.

God knew that no matter how far we strayed from the Garden, we could never abandon it completely. At the deepest level of our being, we had known unconditional love and acceptance. We had forgotten that experience, but in the end, when we were reeling in our deepest pain, we would remember it. We would remember God's love, because it was the essence of who we are.

When we left the Garden, we began a quest for knowledge outside of ourselves. We sought truth in the ideas and philosophies of other people. We read books, traveled to far-away places, sought esoteric and unusual experiences. All this took us away from our inner connection with God. We tried to find outside of us what we already had within. Indeed, the more we sought truth without, the more we forgot the inner connection with truth. Our relationship with God, which once had been intrinsic, became extrinsic. We made idols and worshiped them. The more we searched outside of us, the more empty we felt within. And the more empty we felt, the more our search was fueled.

For some of us God became a large bank account, an exquisite house, or a fancy car. For others it became an expensive education, or a successful career. Still others found idols in a bible, a teaching/belief system, or a preacher/guru. And of course, a few made idols of a bottle, a recreational drug, casual sex, or the promise of love.

All these things seemed to offer us satisfaction, but none of them delivered the love or the comfort they promised. Instead, they left us feeling empty, wanting more and more.

We became overstimulated without and lost our capacity to feel and connect within. Our relationship to love had become inverted. We became needy, dependent, alone. We forgot how to offer love. We could only ask for it.

We desperately wanted relationship, yet we could not handle its demands. We had become too selfish, too defensive. We had driven ourselves into a corner. The very thing we wanted most was the thing we could not have, or at least this is what we believed.

The search for God outside of us led to a wall we could not climb or get around. It was too tall and too wide. We were at an impasse.

The journey outside of ourselves had come to an end. There was nothing left to do but turn around.

To turn authentically, we had to recognize the utter futility of the search for love outside ourselves. That moment of recognition would be the beginning of our spiritual path. It would be the end of our descent from grace, and the beginning of our return to the Garden.

When I return, I look for God the only place I can find the divine: within my own heart and mind. When I look, I see Christ crucified upon a cross. But that Christ is not Jesus. It is me. It is my relentless attack upon myself. In my search for happiness outside myself, I made many enemies. Yet my hatred for them was nothing compared to my hatred for myself. For every problem or trauma I encountered without, I experienced a wound within. Now I see that the tortured one is me. Like Jesus, I too have been crucified.

I thought it was my brother pounding the nails into my hands and feet. But now I know that it was me. Everything I ever did to anyone else, I did to me. I am the victim of my own actions. The executioner does not lie outside of myself.

It is not easy to turn. It is not easy to learn to take total responsibility for our experience. It is not easy to give up the game of shame and blame. Yet, if I want to turn my life around, that is what I am asked to do.

I must look at the hell I have created within my own consciousness and take responsibility for it. I must understand once and for all time that I am the one who walks to the cross, the one who is crucified, and the one who performs the crucifixion. There is no one else here but me.

But if I can wrong myself so completely, if I can torture and abuse myself in this way, if I can be the one who experiences hell itself, can I not also be the one who brings love and compassion. Can I not also be the peacemaker, the Christ, the one who comes with arms extended?

If I can create hell, can I not also create heaven? Is my creativity essentially distorted, prejudiced toward error/evil, or is it simply misdirected? Am I like Adam or Eve, a man or woman condemned to suffer for all eternity for my mistakes, or am I the fallen angel who once sat at God's side, the one suffering from pride who needs but to surrender to regain his celestial seat?

Do I have a choice? Can I create with God, instead of against him?

Lucifer means light bearer. The anointed one is not outside. S/he is mythic. S/he can only be found within.

When I stop crucifying myself, my resurrection is at hand. When I learn to bring love and acceptance to my own wounded psyche, the Christ within steps off the cross and walks free of shame and blame. When I can do that for myself, I can offer the same hand of love to your crucified self. Then we can go home together.

When Adam and Eve overcome their shame and meet face to face, the conditions for the return to the Garden are in place. Each looks at the sins of the other and sees only innocent mistakes. Each knows the time for learning has come. Mistakes do not condemn, nor do they have to be repeated.

When each person takes total responsibility, there is no one left to blame. There is no more enemy to be found outside self, and the enemy within has been forgiven. That is the path back to the garden, the path of forgiveness, the one that Jesus showed us, and the one he offers to us, even now.

Sin and Redemption

When I sat at the kitchen table contemplating suicide in 1973, I did not know that I was responsible for my experience. I thought that I was a victim of pain in a meaningless world. I did not know that my pain belonged to me and was my responsibility to transform. I did not know that I was here with specific lessons to learn about how to love myself and others.

I did not know that life couldn't show up the way I wanted it to as long as I demanded that it be a certain way. My expectations and demands were the cross on which my experience manifested. Until I changed my attitude toward life, everything I experienced would be filled with pain and suffering.

Trying to change the external events and circumstances of life without addressing my internal beliefs and attitudes had proved to be a waste of time. If I wanted change in the outer circumstances of my life, I needed to accept things as they were and begin to look at the contents of my own consciousness. What meaning was I giving to the situation that presented itself? Was I suffering because of what happened or because of my interpretation of it?

The spiritual path begins with self-scrutiny, not with mechanical words and deeds aimed at increasing our ability to get what we want. The search for external abundance cannot succeed when we are feeling bankrupt within, even when it results in increasing our wealth or possessions.

Inner wealth translates into appropriate supply: neither too much nor too little. We have just what we need when we need it.

That is the living experience of the garden. When we are hungry, we reach out and take the fruit from the tree that stands before us. If it's an apple tree, we take the apple. We don't push it away and look for an orange or a grapefruit.

We accept life as it is offered to us, and so avoid an unnecessary struggle. We are in an ongoing dialog with the divine. Inner and outer are in constant communion.

As we stop finding fault with our experience and begin to accept it and work with it, we find that we are getting exactly what we need. We learn to see beyond appearances.

The more we accept life and surrender to it, the more harmonious our experience feels. And we find it increasingly easier to bring a positive attitude toward it. This results in less struggle and greater happiness.

In my own way, I discovered the principle that "thought is creative." The way I look at something influences the way I experience it and what I attract to me in the future. If I stop resisting and struggling, life gets easier. Events which support my life begin to occur naturally. I don't have to try to make them happen.

By accepting what is and cooperating with it, I begin to experience my own creative power. I begin to think, to will, to create "with God" instead of apart from Him.

I take responsibility for my own happiness moment to moment, and stop seeking it outside of me. That changes my experience. I move from seeking without to finding within. And once I find within, I see that mirrored in my life.

The truth is that I can change my experience. But

that change begins with a shifting of my own perceptions. Therefore, it can never be mechanical. My heart must be in it or I am powerless to shift any external condition in my life. The inner work always comes first.

The law of grace operates from the inside out. As changes are made in the way I hold my experience, my experience begins to shift.

When we stop trying to change our experience and accept it, the flow of grace begins. Acceptance says to God: "I accept the reality that presents itself to me, even when it appears to be scary or dark. I open myself to the inner wisdom it brings to me. I open myself to the deepening of my capacity to love and to care."

I do not push my experience away just because it shows up differently from the way I expect it to. When it shows up different from what I expect, I take a deep breath, let go of my expectations, and try to get my arms around what is happening. I know that my job is to embrace everything that happens to me. And that the more difficult it is for me to embrace something, the more deeply I will learn from it.

I learn to stop resisting and to surrender into life. I stop distrusting and begin to trust. In so doing, I shift my consciousness. And as consciousness shifts, so does the external reality that reflects it.

I never know how external reality will shift. I have to keep surrendering my demands and expectations. That is a perpetual process. Surrender just doesn't happen once or twice. It happens continually, day to day, hour to hour, moment to moment.

The outside aligns with the inside. This is a spiritual law. It is the law of grace.

But it can't be quantified. It can't be precisely described. It can't become a technology of transformation.

Consciousness is poetry in motion. It is a dance of form, embodied for a moment and then empty again. It comes into being, changes shape, disappears and reappears. It is playful, spontaneous, always new. You must be in the moment to see it or appreciate it. It has nothing to do with the past or the future.

Understanding what our responsibility is in life is the invitation to the dance. The rest is practice: the dance itself...dancing with self, with other, with life unfolding and the indwelling God.

I received that invitation in 1973. When did you receive it? When did Christ make Itself known to you? When did the voice of the living God speak to you in your time of fear, distrust and pain?

Jesus has told us "knock and it will be open." When we ask for help, we will receive it.

But it never comes unless we ask. Have you asked for help, or are you still trying to do it alone?

It is easier to find the source of Love, when the Friend comes into your life. Have you asked the Friend to join you?

I can tell you that S/he has always been with you, but that will not mean anything to you if you have not learned to ask for help. For lest you ask, S/he cannot appear. And until S/he appears, you will feel that you must do it by yourself.

This is all a game of hide and seek. First I hide and you seek me. Then it is your turn to hide.

The truth is that you are better at hiding than I am at finding you. I am willing to concede. I am willing to end the game. Are you?

The Friend is with us, but we cannot see Him. He leads us beside the still waters. He speaks deeply to our souls. In our communion with Him, we know that goodness and mercy follow us throughout all our nights and our days, and that we will live in His house forever.

In my time of terror and disbelief, the Friend came to me with a booming voice. "There are two worlds," he told me, "the world of pain and the world of surrender, the world of struggle and the world of grace. Choose which world you want to see. For the world you choose to see is the world you will live in.

As you sow, so shall you reap. As you believe, so will your beliefs be embodied."

Part Two
The Teaching

You and God

You have heard me say that "I am the way, the truth and the life." That statement is equally true for you. The truth, the path to the divine, the life of the witness runs through your heart. There is no way, no truth, no life, except through you.

Please understand this. It is the core of my realization and my teaching.

God does not exist apart from you. God is the essence of your being. S/he is the essence of all beings. God dwells within your heart and within the hearts of all beings.

Seeking God

It is not necessary to seek God, because God is already the essence of who you are. To connect with God, simply remove all that separates you from your own essence. Remove all judgments and thoughts that do not bless you and others. These are not your essence. They are false ideas that you carry around. They are the veil, the illusion that appears to separate you from your own heart and the heart of God. Remove the illusions, lift the veil, and you will rest in the heart. Rest in the heart, and God will abide with you.

Open Heart and Mind

When you are judging another or yourself, neither your mind nor your heart is open. When you are complaining, blaming, holding grievances, pushing love away or finding fault with your experience, you are contracted in heart and mind. Behind this contraction is a simple fear that you are somehow unworthy or not good enough.

Becoming aware of your fear is essential if you wish to reconnect to love. You cannot open your heart or your mind as long as your fear remains unconscious. You must bring your fear into conscious awareness.

When you see the fear that underlies your judgments and your attack thoughts, just let it be. Don't beat yourself up for having these thoughts or push the fear away. Just be with the fear and know that it is okay that you are afraid. Tell yourself "I know I'm scared and feeling unworthy. That's why I'm blaming others or finding fault with my life."

Gently take the responsibility away from others: "It's not anyone else's fault that I don't feel good enough. I don't have to project my fear and unworthiness onto someone else. I can look at my fear directly and see that I need to bring some love and acceptance to myself. I can be with my fear in a compassionate way."

When you are able to hold your fear in a compassionate way, you reconnect to your heart. You open your mind. You feel energy as you release others from blame and open to your own love. Your consciousness expands. You stop seeing your situation in a limited way.

Love is the essence of who you are. Everything else that you think or feel about yourself or anyone else is just an illusion. Illusions are born when you stop loving yourself or another. The only way to dissolve illusions is to start loving right now in this moment.

If you want to reconnect with God, Love yourself. Be compassionate with yourself right now. If you want to reconnect with yourself, love the person who is in front of you. When you love another, you can feel compassion for and acceptance of yourself stirring in your heart and mind.

The friend is always there. You have merely to call on him or her.

I am the one who waits within your heart and

mind for acknowledgement. When you acknowledge me, you open your heart to your brother or sister. When you love your brother or sister, you stretch out your hand to me.

The Friend

The friend is the Christ within you. It doesn't matter what you call him or her. The friend is the one who has your greatest good at heart. The friend is the one who also has the greatest good of others at heart.

The friend is the one who is free of judgment, the one who accepts you and everyone else unconditionally. This friend is within every mind and heart. S/he embodies essence. S/he is the voice of God in your experience.

Some people call the Friend Christ. Some call the Friend Buddha, Krishna, or Ram. Names do not matter. The friend is the embodiment of love. S/he has many names and faces.

God and the Friend are always one. When you reach to the Friend within, God hears your footsteps.

In the Beginning

In the beginning was God, Original Presence/ Intention, Indivisible and Boundless Love. In the act of Creation, God expressed His/Her essence in many different ways. Thus, Love became embodied. Out of oneness came diversity.

In every form born of love, the spark of love inheres. In each of the ten thousand things, the original essence remains. Thus, within your heart and mind right now is the original spark of Creation. It belongs to you and can never leave you. No matter where your life takes you, no matter how far you stray from the path, you cannot extinguish the spark of divinity within your own consciousness. It was and is God's gift to you.

You can forget about the gift but you cannot give it back. You can ignore or deny it, but you cannot uncreate it. The deeper the darkness through which you walk, the brighter the tiny spark becomes. It calls to you like a beacon reminding you of your essence and your place of origin.

When you acknowledge the spark and nurture it, the light within you grows. The more attention you give to it, the more the light within you expands.

Soon it seems that your whole being is surrounded by light. Even total strangers feel the rays of your love touching them.

You enter the spiritual path when you acknowledge the spark within and begin to attend to it. That is the moment when you stop being a victim and begin to take full responsibility for your life. The spiritual path culminates when you fully realize your God nature and that of all the other beings around you. Then you too become The Friend, the Christ, the Buddha, the compassionate one.

Attending to the Spark

The spark can be detected only when you are looking for it. It requires a conscious effort. If you live your life reactively, you never notice the spark. You see only the darkness.

To see the spark, you must come to understand that you are not defined by what happens outside of you. Although you have to deal with what happens, you are always free to respond to it creatively. To respond creatively means to choose from a position of strength, from an awareness that you have a number of options.

You cannot respond creatively if you feel attacked

by life. When you feel attacked, you respond reactively and defensively. Victims see very few options, nor do they act from a position of strength.

When you are in touch with the light within, everything that you do is done out of the consciousness of that light. Your actions are empowered by the understanding that the love and the wisdom of God abide within you. You know that you cannot be forsaken by God, regardless of how external reality appears to you.

To be sure, your fear can be triggered. You can forget the light within and see only the darkness before you. You can feel attacked/rejected by others. You can even feel attacked/rejected by God. But all this happens because you look away from the light, instead of toward it.

You look away from God instead of toward Him/Her. Is it any wonder that you feel forsaken or betrayed?

When you look outside for proof that God loves you, you find a mixed bag. Sometimes God seems to favor you and sometimes God seems to have forgotten you exist. But remember, when you look outside, you don't find God, because God isn't out there. God is within. God isn't in how life appears. That's just the veil. To see the truth, you must lift the veil.

God is in the truth of who you are. God isn't the temporal, the changing, the inconstant. God is the eternal, the unchanging, the constant, because God is love and never stops being love.

But if you aren't looking within, you can live your whole life and never know that God exists. You can think that life gave you a raw deal. You can be bitter, resentful, angry. There's nothing to be done about this if you insist on looking outside of yourself for validation or approval.

An about-face is necessary. You must turn to the place where God abides. You must look into your own heart. You must find the place in you which is unconditionally aligned with love.

You can't do this while you are blaming others or holding onto grievances. That is still looking without. Nor can you do it when you are feeling guilty and beating yourself up for making mistakes. That is just taking the veil and putting it on the other side. You must take the veil down completely. All judgment must go. All apparent "knowledge" must be surrendered. You must come to God empty, with open arms. To rest in the heart, you cannot bring your judgments, your interpretations, your fixed ideas. They must be left at the threshold. When you enter the heart you must enter softly, with openness and trust.

You can enter the heart only if you are willing to walk in forgiveness with yourself and others, even if that willingness seems only to be in the moment. That is all God needs anyway...just a moment of your time and attention...just a moment when you drop your defenses and open to the presence of love. It does not matter that you have judged in the past or may judge in the future. All that matters is that right now you are willing to lay your judgments down.

Burning Bush/Bottomless Well

When you know that the Source of Love lies within you, you can leave your worries behind and enter the sanctuary for rest and renewal. Your heart is the place where love is born. It is the bottomless well from which you can draw as often as you need to. Every time you come to the well, you drink the waters of life. Your spiritual thirst is quenched. Your sins are forgiven. You are baptized, healed and renewed.

Whenever life shows up differently from the way you expect it to, whenever the problems of life seem to overwhelm you, there is only one place that offers you sanctuary. You must learn to make your pilgrimage there on a regular basis.

Don't look outside of yourself for answers. Don't seek refuge in the ideas, opinions and advice of other people. Don't go into your head and try to figure things out. Surrender all of that, and seek the place where love begins, in your own heart. It is your responsibility to reconnect with the Source of love when you need to. No one else can do it for you.

It doesn't matter what spiritual practice you do as long as it takes you into your heart and helps you connect with the Source of Love. If it does that, then stay with it throughout all the twists and turns of your life. Hold to your practice. It is your lifeline. When storms come up unexpectedly, it keeps you afloat. Ever so gradually, it brings you home.

When the spark in your heart is attended to, it grows into a steady flame. When the flame is fed by acts of loving kindness to self and others, it becomes a blazing fire, a source of warmth and light for all who encounter it. When Moses saw the Burning Bush, he knew that it was God revealing Himself. What he did not know was that Bush was not in the world, but in the heart.

I am the Way

I am the way not because I am special but because I have aligned with Love, the essence of my being. You too can align with Love.

I ask you to look to my example, not because I want you to worship me or put me on a pedestal, but because I want you to understand what is possible for you. I am the mentor, the model. I not only speak the truth; I also embody It.

When I said "I am the Way," I wanted you to go beyond just hearing my words. I wanted you to see how the word became flesh, how what I taught was demonstrated in my life. I wanted you to realize that I offered you a living teaching, not just a set of abstract beliefs. I wanted you to know that to follow me meant more than preaching my words. It meant following my example.

There is nothing special about who I am or what I have done. If you insist on calling me "Lord," do not do so out of envy or littleness, but out of the awareness that this same "Lord" you see in me is within you. If you call me Rabbi, do so because you see the light which is in you made manifest in my presence. Power is not separately vested in me or in you, but it abides in what we experience together when our hearts are open.

Love Your Neighbor as Yourself

I have asked you to see me as a brother, because I am your absolute equal. I have asked you to see one another as brothers and sisters for the same reason.

As soon as there is the slightest perception of inequality between any of us, we must understand that we have left our hearts. We have abandoned the truth.

Let us not justify our thoughts or actions of separation, but acknowledge that we are not in our right mind, and return to the consciousness of mutual acceptance and inclusion. Let us cease from thinking and acting in ways that do not honor self and other equally.

I have told you many times that your good and that of your brother or sister are one and the same. You cannot advance your life by hurting another, nor can you help another by hurting yourself. All attempts to break this simple equation lead to suffering and despair.

If you wish to prosper, love your neighbor. Care for her happiness in the same way that you would care for your own. For in honoring her, you will honor the divine in yourself and thus strengthen your love and your faith.

Love Even Your Enemy

Even those who oppose you deserve your love and your blessings. They are your absolute equals too. You cannot love me and hate them. If you hate them, then you offer me the same hatred.

There is no brother or sister who is unworthy of my love. If there were one such, then my awakening would not be complete. That is why I have told you that there are no exceptions to the law of equality. If you would condemn any one of my brothers or sisters or withhold your love from them, then you are not following my teaching or my example.

Turn the Other Cheek

I have advised you that if someone injures you, you should not attack back, but instead turn the other cheek. Turning the other cheek does not mean that you condone the attack or that you are inviting the other person to attack you again. Quite the contrary, by turning the other cheek, you are inviting your brother or sister to make a different choice. You are not holding onto the past and using the past to condemn your brother or sister in this moment. You are holding open the possibility that the choice made in this moment can be a different one.

When you understand that every attack is a call for love, you begin to realize that your response to attack can totally transform it. Someone attacks you out of fear and unworthiness, and you respond with the love you know that person needs. That offers the person a choice s/he did not know s/he had before.

The reality is that people will attack you. And you will attack them. And it will be for the same reason. Neither one of you feels worthy of love and you mistakenly think that the other person is blocking your access to the love you want. In fact, the other person is the doorway to the love that you want. Your enemy is your ally in disguise. If you offer your enemy love, you will make peace with yourself.

When someone responds to your attack with acceptance, compassion and love, how can you attack them again? When they refuse to take offense, and just want you to see who they really are, how can you refuse to see?

All attack happens because we dehumanize the object of our attack. We make that person "less than we are." In this way, we justify our attack. But the justification is always false because it violates the law of equality. We are never justified in attacking anyone.

While you may refuse to condone a person's actions toward you, you should not cast that person out of your heart. Give him an opportunity to make a different choice. Support that choice by offering him the love and the respect that will inspire him to engage in caring, responsible actions in the future.

To turn the other cheek does not mean that you refuse to stand up against injustice. Quite the contrary. I encourage you to oppose injustice wherever you encounter it. Take issue with actions that are uncaring, hurtful, disrespectful to yourself or others, but do so in a loving way. Do so in a way that respects the people whose actions you oppose. For they are your brothers and sisters too.

Your proper attitude toward all people should be one of mutual respect. However much you might take issue with others, they remain your equals. Their opinions, beliefs, values, likes or dislikes are as important as your own. Offer respect and ask for it in return. It is your birthright.

Innocence and Guilt

The part of you that condemns another person is the part of you that feels unworthy. If you felt worthy, you would not judge or attack others. You would see the pain that underlies their hostility and feel compassion for them.

When you are established in your own innocence, you know that no one, no matter how terribly they act toward you, can take your worthiness away. You know in the depths of your being that you are lovable. Nothing happening outside of you can challenge that internal conviction. That is why I could look on my crucifiers with compassion. When I said "Forgive them, Father, for they know not what they do," it was the absolute truth. They did not know.

The executioner sees the unworthiness of his victim, but he cannot see his own unworthiness, for to see it would undermine his ego structure, his false strength, his fearful compact with the crowd. To see his own unworthiness would take him into the depths of despair. Is it any wonder that most people turn away from the confrontation with the shadow within and instead project it onto others?

It is always easier to blame others and attack them

than it is to acknowledge our fears and our mistakes. It is always easier to see our enemy outside than to confront the enemy within. To acknowledge the disowned aspects of self and bring them into conscious awareness, to accept and love the parts of ourselves that we judge, hate or feel guilty about is a far more challenging task.

Yet the truth is that we don't begin to walk the spiritual path until we are willing to take responsibility for bringing healing and wholeness to our own psyche. Spirituality happens from the inside out. It happens as we learn to love and accept ourselves at deeper and deeper levels of being.

As long as we are trying to change or fix something outside of ourselves, we continue to hide our pain and our guilt. Our professed spiritual beliefs are like a bandaid covering a festering wound. It is only a matter of time until the wound must be addressed.

Born Again in Grace

We begin the path of ascension when we hit bottom and come face to face with the depth of our self-judgment and fear. We take our first few steps on the way to wholeness when we stop acting like a victim and blaming others for our pain, when we know that our healing has very little to do with anyone else; it's mainly about our relationship with our self.

We begin to surrender to love when we become willing to feel our pain and move through it. We become vulnerable, accessible, willing to be present and feel whatever we are feeling. Our hearts begin to open.

To be reborn in spirit means that we finally know without any doubt that our responsibility is to love and honor ourselves and others. We commit to love and forgiveness not just as ideas, but as a way of life. We agree to treat others as equals, to hold their good equally with our own.

To be born again means that we understand that God has never abandoned us. We simply turned away from God in our pain, our fear, our guilt and our feelings of unworthiness. In a real sense, we abandoned ourselves.

In our fall from Grace, each one of us forsakes the light within. We create ourselves in our own image, instead of understanding how we are reflections of the Divine. We rely on our ego structures to meet our perceived needs and, without the inner light guiding us, we experience life as hardship and struggle. Even easy tasks become difficult.

Grace does not come from without but from

within. It comes through our inner alignment with Spirit. When we are in constant dialogue with all parts of ourselves, we learn to honor ourselves more completely. We do not commit to activities about which we are ambivalent or have misgivings. We learn to listen to ourselves — all of who we are — more deeply, so that when we act we do so from a profound integrity.

Because we wait for integration and clarity within, our outer actions create harmony, instead of conflict. Our lives seem to slow down and become more spacious. We are less anxious and pressured. We do less, but what we do is far more effective than what we did before when we were under pressure to decide before we were ready.

By honoring ourselves, we also honor others. We don't give mixed messages. We don't make promises we are unable to keep.

None of this would be possible if we had been unwilling to face our fears. Grace cannot come from the denial of the shadow side. It can't come from resisting life or pushing away parts of ourselves we don't want to face. Grace comes from the integration of dark and light, from the inner marriage of male and female, heart and mind, wounded child and spiritual adult.

Grace is the movement from inner wholeness to outer wholeness. Sin or Karma is the movement from inner conflict to outer conflict. When the spiritual adult aligns with the wounded child, Karmic conditions are dissolved, for the division within consciousness ceases to be.

All healing happens thus: As illusions are surrendered, truth appears. As separation is relinquished, the original unity emerges unchanged. When we stop pretending to be what we are not, what we are can be clearly seen.

The second birth is the letting go of all that is false (personality) so that our true spiritual identity can be experienced. It is the letting go of our prejudice and conditioning so that which is unbiased and unconditional can be welcomed into our lives.

Grace happens when we abide with what is. Struggle happens when we push what is away or try to bring something else in. Grace happens when we accept. Struggle happens when we reject or try to fix. Grace is natural. Struggle is unnatural. Grace is effortless. Struggle is efforting.

Grace is "with" God. Struggle is "without" God. We have tried it both ways and we have seen the results of each way demonstrated. There is no question which way feels the best. Yet we keep mistaking one way for the other. We keep mistaking the voice of ego for the voice of Spirit. We keep getting in the way.

When we are in the way, we suffer. We know that we are not in our right place. That is when we must acknowledge our mistake and move out of the way.

When we stay out of the way, we are an empty channel, a willing instrument for the divine. Grace flows through us. God's will expresses through our lives. We don't get the credit, but we do experience the energy of love as it moves through us.

In the end, we must decide what is most important to us. Do we want the credit, the ego reinforcement or the acceptance and the love? One makes us important in the eyes of the world. The other helps us stay humble and in equal relationship with others.

Crucifixion and Resurrection

We think our actions condemn us for all time. We think that God is vengeful and will punish us for our mistakes. But that is not the God I know. That is the God created out of human fear and guilt.

The God I know and serve shows us how to learn from our mistakes. The God I know forgives and encourages us to make loving restitution toward those we have injured.

You think that I died for your sins. That is a total misunderstanding of my life and my teaching. I came to teach that no sin is unforgivable, that every being deserves love, including those who strike out against others in their fear and their pain. I did not die to save you from your sins, nor did I die to condemn you for crucifying me. I died, quite simply, because you could not recognize me in yourself.

You, my friend, will die for the same reason. Even now, you do not recognize me — the anointed one — within yourself. My resurrection is but the symbol and promise of that recognition. It does not matter whether or not I took my physical body with me into the light. What matters is that, in the total recognition of the light, bodies become insignificant. When love is present, we no longer need to know or understand how we are different from one another.

In our resurrection in the light, life and death become one and the same. There is no life except in the death or relinquishment of all that separates us from love or interferes with our embodiment of it.

I do not wish to make this esoteric or complicated. Suffice it to say that I am not the only one who has been crucified, nor am I the only one who will be resurrected from the prison of pain. My passion play is just a metaphor for your own.

Blessing or Curse?

It is the intention that you hold that really matters. Do you intend to bless or to curse, to accept or to find fault? If you intend to bless and to accept, then more often than not you will succeed. And when you do make a mistake, you will acknowledge it and try to learn from it.

Every moment is new. It doesn't matter what happened yesterday or last year. It doesn't even matter what just happened. Right now you have a new choice to make.

What is your intention in this moment? Is it to bless or to curse? Were you so injured by what just happened or by what happened years ago that right now you insist on holding onto your grievances? Have you released the past or are you still holding onto it?

When your intention is to bless, you cannot hold onto the past. You must let it go to be open to this moment. And if you are not open to this moment, then how can you accept it and offer it your cooperation, your blessing?

If you have closed your heart or your mind, you cannot bless. You can only judge, blame, complain or condemn. So ask yourself what your intention is. Are you here to bless or to judge? And if you want to judge, just be aware of it. Just be aware: "I am still carrying a past hurt, a past wound. I am not ready to bless."

Let the awareness "I am not ready to bless" be present. Realize that whatever you say or do in this moment will be a judgment or attack, because you are not ready to bless. In this moment, all you can do is be with your fear, your hurt, your anger, your judgment.

Admit "In this moment I can only be with my fear, because I am not ready to bless." That's the truth of what's happening and there's no harm done. There's no harm when you refrain from speaking or acting when you are upset. There is just the experience of being present for yourself in your pain and feelings of separation.

When you can be with yourself in this way, you bring love in. The more love you bring in, the more you begin to accept and to bless yourself and your experience. And before long, you are ready to extend that blessing to others.

Whose job is it to weather these moments of separation when you feel cut off from others or from God? Is it not your job? How can you make it any one else's responsibility?

So you ask: "Do I intend to bless or to curse?" and you become aware of your intention. And if your intention is to bless, then you know that your words and actions will be helpful. And if your intention is not to bless, then you know that nothing you say or do can be helpful now.

Our spiritual goal is to know that everything we think, feel or do is coming from love. If it is coming from love, it will be a loving thought, a loving feeling, a loving action. We will be instruments of love and understanding in the world. If it is not coming from love, then we will be sowing seeds of strife.

When we are at peace, we do not create conflict. We extend peace. When we are clear, we do not create confusion. We extend clarity.

Whatever is within us will be expressed outside of us. This is the law of manifestation. If we want different outer results, we must take care of what we harvest within. To take care requires awareness of our intention in each moment.

To refrain from speaking or acting when one is not ready to bless interrupts the karmic flow. Manifestation cannot happen as long as we dwell in silent awareness of our own inner states. By so doing, we take responsibility for the contents of our own consciousness. We do not project our discomfort onto others.

In the same manner, when someone else projects onto us, blaming us for their pain or discomfort, we must take care not to react to their accusations. They are not in their right mind. If we react, we too will not be in our right mind.

That is why it is important to listen with compassion to another person's cry for attention and for love. When we listen with compassion, we don't feel attacked, even though we know the other person is trying to blame us. We just tune into how much pain the person feels and how difficult it is for him or her to face that pain. We don't accept the blame another person places at our feet, but we don't try to defend ourselves either. The person is simply mistaken about us. We know that. And we stand lovingly in the truth of who we are.

When we are coming from love, we listen without judgment to other people. We empathize with their pain and encourage them to value themselves. Because we don't take offense when people inappropriately blame us, we refuse to be targets for their projections. We don't engage their pain with our pain, their anger with our anger, or their unworthiness with our own. We mirror back to them their innocence by refusing to make anyone guilty.

By speaking and acting only when we are able to bless, we stand free of the painful drama of mutual trespass and betrayal. We take care of ourselves and others at the deepest level of being. Waves of illusion wash over us, but we stand simply and firmly in the truth of who we are.

Holding on to the Love

We come into relationship to one another in different ways: as children, parents, siblings, friends, workmates, teachers, students. What is important is not the form of the relationship, but the love that abides within the form.

Relationships constantly change form. Children grow up and become parents, parents surrender their bodies to the next adventure, friends move apart, lovers break up, and so it goes. No form remains the same.

Growth must continue. Forms must come and go. That is the bittersweet quality of life. If we become attached to the form or throw away the love just because the form is changing, we will suffer unnecessarily. The challenge is to let the form go, but hold onto the love.

To love another is a spiritual act. It is an unconditional gesture. When I love you now, there is no limit placed on that love. It is timeless and eternal. When you feel my love in this moment, you don't have to be concerned for the next moment, because love naturally extends. It continues to be itself. If it is here now, it will be here always. Love does not change. The form that love takes will change, but love itself will not change. It will simply find a new form for expression.

Too often we deny the love we have for one another when the form changes. That is just another kind of attachment to form. It says: "I must have love in this particular way or I do not want it at all." That is childish. When we grow up, we realize that we can't always have things exactly the way we want them, especially when other people are involved.

When one person no longer wants to keep an agreement, the agreement is off. You can't hold another person against his or her will. If you try to do so, you will push love away. Love survives the ending of agreements, if you will allow it to.

Love and freedom go hand in hand. Love cannot be contained in a specific form. It must break free of all forms, all conditions, if it is to become itself fully. Resisting this organic process just creates separation.

Grant to the other person the freedom to be who s/he is and the form will take care of itself. Try to take away that freedom and the form will become a prison for both of you.

True relationship happens only among people who regard each other as equals. It happens only among those who honor and respect one another. It happens only when people are present for each other right now.

If love is present now, then we need take no thought for the future. We need to think about the future only when we aren't fully present right now.

When we are in harmony with one another now, no plans or external agreements are necessary. Why would they be? When there is complete trust, the absence of trust is an abstract and irrelevant proposition.

When love is lacking, then we want guarantees about love. When love is here, guarantees are not necessary.

Everything comes into being right now. All creation is happening now. The alpha and omega of existence are present in this moment. There will never be more love than is possible here and now.

Do you hear that? The greatest love that we can attain is attainable right now. It cannot be experienced in the past and future.

The attachment to form is about the past or the future. It is never about now. When love is present now, form is irrelevant. If I love you now, it does not matter what you look like, what you are saying, or how you act. It just matters that I love you, that I accept you, that I feel connected to you. And if you feel my love and acceptance, then you have the freedom to be however you need to be in that moment. When you can be yourself without being concerned about losing my love or jeopardizing our connection, then your angelic nature can be realized.

When we hold onto the love, we become its embodiment. Forms may change, but we continue to love one another through all those changes.

Love and freedom are inseparable. I cannot love you if I do not have the choice.

All forms of bondage are assaults not just on freedom, but on love itself. Because love cannot exist when we lose the freedom to choose.

The great tragedy of love is not that we may choose not to be together. That is sad perhaps, but not tragic. The real tragedy is that we may stay together or separate because we believe we have no other choice. If there is love, there must be the freedom to choose a form that works for both of us. And to do that we must hold onto our love for one another and let the form go when it no longer serves our highest good.

This takes courage. It takes heart. It takes patience. But that is the nature of love. And those who love each other through all the conditions, all the ups and downs of life, are patient and courageous beyond measure.

Facing Your Fears

You know that when you stay with how you think and feel right in the moment, it is not difficult to be present for what comes up. But as soon as present events trigger the wounds of the past, it is easy to feel overwhelmed.

When this happens, it is important to see that the past is coming up for healing. Much of what you feel belongs to you. It is your history, your drama, your interpretation of what is happening. If you try to make it someone else's responsibility, you will needlessly complicate your relationship with that person.

Share what is coming up for you with others, but

don't even hint that they are in any way responsible for it. Your anxiety and pain is not caused by other people. It is a condition of your own consciousness.

Take responsibility for what belongs to you. Own it, look at it, and let it go. Let the fears of the past be resolved in the present. Acknowledge them, but do not allow them to possess you. The demons of the past will hold you in bondage forever if you let them.

Don't give the past power over your present. Invite the past into the here and now and face your fears directly, once and for all. Once you know what your fear is, take responsibility for it, and acknowledge it to yourself and others, you are finished with it. If it should come up again, you just re-cognize it: "Oh, you are back again. What do you want?" And you listen to the voice of fear as a parent listens to a scared child. You are compassionate with that child but very clear that these fears are without substance. This comforts the child and s/he feels safe.

Imagine, though, what would happen if the parent was spooked by the child's fear. Then there would be no way that the child would feel safe.

Please understand that there are scared, maybe even terrified voices within you. You can't ignore them or they will reach out and grab your attention when you least expect them to. Nor can you afford to empower those fears or they will rampage within you. Instead, you acknowledge them and lovingly let them go.

When I was in the desert for forty days, I experienced every voice of fear you can imagine. These were not devils outside of me that had come to tempt me. They were voices in my own mind that caused me to doubt myself or others.

You too have your time in the desert when you must face your own fears and doubts. This time of inner testing always precedes your accepting your life purpose here. For if you cannot move through your own fears, how can you begin to deal with the fears of others when they project them onto you? Remember, those who are full of light attract the most attention.

If you are not whole and strong in yourself, how can you be a beacon of love and light for others? The kind of strength and integration I am talking about here is not to be taken lightly. Can you meet your devils and learn to love them? Can you listen to the scared voices within your mind and reassure them? Can you affirm that you are worthy in the midst of a steady stream of thoughts about your unworthiness? Can you believe in your love when the hurt children of your mind tell you that love is an illusion and that you had better learn to defend yourself better? Can you love when fear comes up? Can you be steady in your re-cognition of the truth of who you are?

These are the critical questions. Before you begin your life work, these questions must be answered. You must enter the darkness of your own psyche carrying the light of awareness. Every fear which undermines your self esteem must be faced. Unless you are strong enough to face your fears and hold them compassionately, you cannot take your appointed place in the scheme of things.

Don't be surprised if your commitment to self is tested when your life purpose is revealed to you. Do not take this as a sign that something is wrong. Nothing is wrong. It is simply time to demonstrate that you are ready. While it may seem that you are trying to convince someone outside yourself, this is not true. You are proving everything to yourself. You are the only one who needs to be convinced.

When you know without a doubt that you are worthy, when you are willing to trust yourself completely, then your purpose on this planet can unfold. Then you can emerge from the desert, having discovered the oasis, the bottomless well of love and compassion which rests beneath the shifting sands of your fear.

The Dance of Acceptance

So much of your life you spend judging yourself and others. Imagine what it would be like to affirm and bless all that you now judge or find wanting.

It is a radical act to accept what happens in your life exactly as it is. When you do that, you stop questioning the validity of your experience.

Your challenge lies in being with your experience or, when you can't be with it, in being aware of your resistance, your judgments, your negative interpretations of it. Being aware of the thoughts that separate you from life creates a bridge back to simple acceptance of the moment as it unfolds.

When you see your resistance, you don't judge it. You don't beat yourself up. You just notice your fear without judgment. When you identify fear, it no longer has the ability to run your life. When you notice your own fear, you no longer react to life out of that fear.

Acceptance is a life-long dance. We get better at it the more we do it. But we never dance perfectly. Fear and resistance continue to come up and we do the best we can with them. Sometimes they slow us down, but slowing down might be exactly what is needed. In the dance of acceptance, unconscious becomes conscious. Your fear becomes your partner.

You dance with the inside and outside situation. You dance with what happens and with what you think and feel about it. The inner and outer dance are going on all the time. There is never a time when you can get off the dance floor and go and take a nap.

The Tao never ceases. Even in our stillness there is movement. The stream never stops flowing. If it is not visible on the surface, then it continues underground.

We live in a dynamic universe...always moving, always changing. Sometimes we get tired and we want to get off the merry-go-round. "I shall dance no more," we self-righteously proclaim. But then, unexpectedly, we fall in love, or someone makes us a business offer we can't refuse. As soon as we really understand that the Emperor has no clothes, his designer shows up with the latest fashions.

No matter how hard we try, we cannot get out of the drama. We can't stop the dance. It goes on with us or without us. That's why our only hope of having a harmonious experience is to learn to move with the flow instead of against it.

When you accept the eternal nature of the dance, it is easier to accept its specific content in the moment. That content may be that you are having a panic attack, yelling at your husband or kids, drinking too much, or even contemplating suicide, but as long as you know that it's part of the dance you can come out of it. You never step into something you can't step out of, no matter how difficult it seems. That's one of the laws of the dance. When you take a false step, you take a breath and keep moving. When you lose the rhythm, you listen for a moment to the music and pick it up again.

Mistakes are part of the dance. But some people don't know this. Their business fails or their partner leaves them and they blow their brains out. They play for very high stakes. They think the dance is about success or failure, black or white. In fact, it's about both, constantly. The dance is a dance of the opposites, a play of contradictions. It is paradoxical. It has always been paradoxical.

One of the greatest paradoxes is this one: You can't be in the dance if you are trying to figure it out! If you are always thinking about how to move your feet, you are going to have a very hard time dancing. But if you just move your feet, you will be dancing. You may not be doing the dance someone else is doing, but you will be dancing your dance. And your dance is as good as anyone's.

The greatest act of acceptance is to know that

what happens is perfect for you. You are not given more than can you handle, nor is anything lacking in your life. To be sure, you can look at your neighbor's yard and think the grass is greener. Maybe he has a bigger house and a nicer car. But you can't see what that means to him. You can't see if he's happy about his house or his car. You can only see if you are happy about it.

And, if you are not happy about it, then you can be sure you are feeling unworthy and unappreciated. And so that is what you must dance with. When you are not accepting your life as it is, you must dance with your lack of acceptance. You must learn to be with your resistance, your envy, your jealousy in a loving way. And that's quite an extraordinary dance.

The more unhappy you are, the harder the dance becomes, because you must dance with your unhappiness. That's why acceptance is so important as a spiritual practice. The more you accept your life as it is, the easier the dance becomes.

Rules Vs. Guidance

Everyone wants rules to live by. But most rules are not helpful. They can too easily be used to persecute others.

The truth is that you do not know what is good for others. Indeed, you often do not know what is good for you. The humility that results from this understanding is essential to living a spiritual life.

Since what you say and do can be helpful or hurtful to others, it is better to remain neutral than to speak or act without insight and understanding. Don't wave your Bibles, your Sutras, your holy books in front of people. Don't insist that they live the way you think they should live. If you are concerned about them, love them. Don't try to convert them. This is not how the teaching extends.

If you have chosen a path, live that path. Demonstrate that you are capable of speaking and acting in a loving, compassionate way. This will get people's attention much more than preaching will.

Your job is not to preach to others, but to find the way to the truth of your heart. You alone know what course of action is best for the fulfillment of your purpose here. But that knowledge is often buried deeply in the heart. Sometimes, it takes a lot of listening to connect with your own wisdom. In some cases, connecting to yourself is not possible until you stop listening to what other people think you should do.

But your responsibility doesn't end here. Once you have heard the voice of your heart, you still have to listen to it. You still have to act in a manner consistent with it. And that might mean taking some risks. It might mean shifting your priorities.

Your inner wisdom will not keep you in a rut. It will bring out the towtruck so you can stop spinning your wheels and get back on the road of your life. But first you have to sign the permission slip. First, you have to be willing.

There is always some kind of payoff in staying stuck. Do you know what yours is? Do you prefer the certainty of prison to the wide open spaces of the world? At least you know where you will sleep and what times your meals will be ready.

When you are used to living by other people's rules, it can seem overwhelming to set your own priorities and make your own decisions. You don't know whether you can handle the responsibility. But if you don't learn to take responsibility for your life, who will? If you don't find your purpose and follow it, how will you find fulfillment?

You can spend your life working for other people and living by their rules, but it won't help you find your path. You must "leave your nets" before you get caught in them.

Working for others should at best be a temporary proposition. Work for others while you learn the skills that you need to work for yourself. Live by other people's rules until the opportunity presents itself for you to act on your own priorities.

Your life must be progressive. You must keep taking the next step.

Be faithful to your ideals. Follow your beliefs. Prove them out. Show yourself and others that they work. Be a beacon of love and compassion. Empower others to find their own truth.

This is how the work extends....Not by preaching. Not by telling people what you think is good for them or allowing them to prescribe for you.

If you look carefully, you will notice that those who have the greatest need to tell others what to do have the least faith in themselves. They haven't even begun to hear the voice in their own hearts; yet they are up on a soapbox telling others what to do.

Such is the absurdity of false witness. When you are in a rut and you are too afraid to step out of it, the first thing you do is try to attract some company. It is not uncommon to build a temple over a ditch and call it God's sanctuary.

I have told you many times to be careful. Things are not always as they seem. Wolves are disguised in sheep's clothing. Prisons of fear and judgment masquerade as temples of love and forgiveness. It helps to keep your eyes open. Don't join the crusade until you see the fruits of people's actions. Words are often cheap and misleading.

If each of you would nurture the truth within your hearts, you would collectively give birth to a very different world. It would be a world of realization, not sacrifice, a world of equality not prejudice, a world of insight and respect, not collusion and despair.

Nobody else can take responsibility for living your life. Not your parents, or your partner, or your children. Not your church, your friends, or your support network. You alone must do it. Does this seem to be a lonely proposition? Well, perhaps in some way it is. But no more exciting task will ever come into your life.

So don't make rules for other people. That will just take the focus away from your life. Let others find their own way. Support them. Encourage them. Cheer them on. But don't think you know what's good for them. You don't know. Nor will you ever know. A co-dependent preoccupation with the lives of others keeps you from taking responsibility for your own life.

Stay in your life. Stay in your heart. Everything that you need to fulfill your destiny will be found within. Listen to your guidance, honor it, act on it, be committed to it, and it will unfold. When you are joined with your own divine nature, the doors you need to walk through will open to you.

The Open Door

Life has its own rhythm. If you are surrendered, you will find it. But surrendering is not so easy.

Surrendering means meeting each moment as new. And to do that, you cannot be attached to what just happened. You can appreciate it. You can savor it. But you must let it go where it will.

You can't control what happens. You can only be open to it or resist it. If you have expectations, you will be resisting. Don't resist. Don't have attachments to the past or expectations of the future.

Just be where you are. Bring everything into the now. Bring the attachment, the expectations into the present. Be aware of your resistance. See the drama of your disappointment. See that you did not get what you wanted. See how it makes you feel. Watch it. Experience it. But don't lose yourself in the drama.

When you can see the drama without reacting to it, you can stay anchored in the here and now. You can remain present. You can see which doors are closed and which ones are open.

Please, don't try to walk through closed doors. You will hurt yourself unnecessarily. Even if you don't know why a door is closed, at least respect the fact that it is. And don't struggle with the doorknob. If the door was open, you would know it. Wanting it to be open does not make it open.

Much of the pain in life is as a result of people attempting to walk through closed doors or trying to put square pegs in round holes. We try to hold onto someone who is ready to go, or we try to get some-body to do something before s/he is ready. Instead of accepting what is and working with it, we inter-fere with it or try to manipulate it to meet our perceived needs.

Obviously, this doesn't work. When we interfere with what is, we create strife for ourselves and oth-ers. We trespass. We get in the way.

That is why awareness is necessary. When we know that things are not flowing, we need to step back and realize that our actions are not helpful. We need to stop, pause, and consider. We need to cease what we are doing because it is not working and we don't want to make the situation worse than it is.

Stopping the offensive action is the first step in the process of At-One-ment for our trespasses. Unless we stop, violation continues. The door stays shut.

After stopping, we acknowledge our mistake, first to ourselves and then to others. Then we vow not to repeat our mistake again.

This is the forgiveness process in its most simple terms. We become aware of our mistake and learn from it so that we do not have to repeat it.

When we interfere in the natural order of things, there is suffering. As soon as we stop interfering, suffering stops.

It is a simple movement from dis-ease to ease, from discomfort to comfort, from disharmony to harmony. We don't need to make the forgiveness process difficult or esoteric. It is a natural, organic process.

When the door is closed, we cannot enter. We must wait patiently or move along and see if another door will open. As long as we are forgiving ourselves and others for our mistakes, there is a good chance that the right door will open. Only when we refuse to learn from our mistakes or hold onto our grievances does it seem that the doors are repeatedly closed to us.

Fortunately, God does not hold grievances. Nor does S/he punish us for our mistakes. God keeps saying to us: "that didn't work too well, did it? Next time, perhaps, you can make a different choice."

It isn't helpful to obsess about our mistakes and feel bad about them. Guilt doesn't help us act more responsibly toward others. But learning from our mistakes does help us take greater responsibility and move on with more harmony and integrity. That's what it means to atone.

Guilt does not contribute to atonement. If anything, it impedes it.

When something does not work, a correction must be made. Adjustments of this kind are a natural part of living in a harmonious way. We can't be right all of the time. We are going to make mistakes, but if we can acknowledge and correct these mistakes, then we can stay on track. The doors will keep opening to us.

Grace comes when correction is constant. Fulfillment happens when we don't just talk about forgiveness, but live it moment to moment. Then, it does not matter how many times we stray from the path or put our feet in our mouths. We can laugh at our errors and put them behind us.

You cannot fit through the door if you are carrying the past around. Don't feel guilty. Instead, take responsibility for correcting your mistakes. That way you don't carry around a lot of excess baggage. The more responsibility you take for your thoughts, feelings, and experiences, the lighter you travel and the easier it is to correct for your mistakes.

Guilt is not constructive. If there is nothing you can do to make the situation better, then just accept it as it is. Sometimes, there's nothing to be done. It's no one's fault. Life is just as it is. And that's okay.

In knowing that life is okay, no matter how ragged and unfinished it seems, there is room for movement. A shift can happen. A door can open.

The most important door is the one to your heart. Is it open or closed? If it is open, then the whole universe abides in you. If it is closed, you stand alone, holding the world off. Trust and the river flows through your heart. Distrust and a dam holds the river back.

A heart in resistance gets tired quickly. Life wears heavily upon it. But a heart that is open is filled with energy. It dances and sings.

When the door in your heart is open, all the important doors open in the world. You go where you need to go. Nothing interferes with your purpose or your destiny. Everything that you are unfolds naturally in its own time, without struggle or restraint. The unexpected happens without difficulty. Miracles are everyday occurrences.

Walking the Tightrope

While it sometimes seems as if we know nothing at all about anything, this is not an accurate statement. We don't know nothing. We know a little bit. Maybe, at times, when we are especially attuned, we know a little bit more.

We never see the whole picture. That is for sure. The more attached we are, the less we see. The more invested we are in a particular outcome, the harder it is for us to accept "what is" and work with it.

To see and accept "what is," we must ask "What do I know right now in this moment?" NOT "What would I like to know?" but "what do I really know to be true right now in my heart?" To see and accept "what is," we must sink down through all the levels of mind that would project this moment into the future, that would scheme and dream and try to take control. We must get through all that mindstuff to the real feeling-core of our being.

Some things belong to the past, not to the present. What happened in the past can prejudice us toward what is happening now. It can constrict us so that we don't open fully to the present. If we can acknowledge our fear about getting hurt, we can put these thoughts aside. We can say "okay, I may have made a mistake in the past, but I can learn from it. I can be more careful this time. I don't have to relive the past." Acknowledging the past and then putting it aside is essential to being in the present.

Some things belong to the future, not to the present. The truth is that we don't know specifically what will happen in the future. To try to know can be very dysfunctional. It can put unnecessary pressure on the present moment. We may have a general sense of the future, based on the way the present is unfolding. We may know what the next step is. But that's about all we can know right now.

To be in the present, we need to stay centered in what we know and put the past and the future aside. We may not know a lot, but we do know something, and we must find a way to live from that place and honor it.

If we keep bringing the past in or trying to plan for the future, we will move out of what we do know. We will start getting behind or ahead of ourselves. We will sow the seeds of conflict within and without.

So this is a balancing act. We need to walk the tightrope between the past and the future. And we can't expect to walk without tipping to one side or the other. But when we do, we must lean the other way, so that we can come back to center, so that we can come back to what we really know and let go of what we don't know.

We don't know, for example, that the past is going to repeat itself. We don't know that our present experience is going to be the same in the future. Things may change or they may stay the same. Old patterns may dissolve or they may reappear. We don't know these things. All we know is how we feel about what's happening right now.

If we can stay with this, then we can be in the present and be honest with ourselves and others about our experience. We can say what we are able to commit to and what we cannot commit to.

Things may change in the future, but we can't live right now hoping it is going to change. We must be where we are, not where we want to be.

This is difficult work. So much of our mindstuff is fear-based. It is resisting "what is" or trying to change it. If we don't move through this resistance to a deeper level of self-attunement, we won't be able to claim the present moment. We will get lost in a reactive buzzsaw of conflicting thoughts and emotions.

The past is saying "Don't open. It's too scary. Don't you remember what happened when...?" and the future is saying "This is taking so long, why don't we just jump in and do it?" The past is trying to hold us back and the future is trying to rush us, an interesting dilemma don't you think?

The truth is that we need to listen to both voices and reassure them that they have been heard. Then, we can rebalance and come back to center. Then, we can try to find a pace that feels good for right now.

That is what the tightrope walker must do. She can't worry about losing her balance in the past. She can't dream about a perfect performance in the future. She needs to focus on what's happening right now. She needs to put one foot in front of the other. Every step is an act of balance. Every step is a spiritual act.

Fortunetelling

Many people want to know what is going to happen to them in the future. They go to psychics, astrologers, tarot card readers and so forth, hoping to hear something that will make them feel better.

The absurdity of this can only be appreciated when you know that the future cannot be predicted. True, there are lines of force emanating from a person's consciousness. There are patterns that are set in motion. But every moment offers us a new choice and that choice alters our destiny. Unfortunately, the more preoccupied we are in finding out what will happen to us in the future, the less attention we can give to the choices we need to make now. That is why a fascination with fortunetelling is discouraged in many spiritual traditions.

The obsession some people have with the past can be just as dysfunctional as this preoccupation with the future. Many people go to therapists or psychics looking for knowledge of the past which could explain problems in the present. They engage in a variety of forms of psychoanalysis, dream therapy, inner child work, hypnotherapy, past life regression and so forth. While this work may help some people move on in their lives, it becomes a quagmire for others. A tool meant to help becomes a dogma. A technique meant to assist us in discovering the source of our pain becomes an invitation to wallow in it and become its perpetual victim.

When we emerge from such therapies with stories about childhood trauma or abuse, or memories of previous lifetimes, we would do well to ask ourselves if these stories help us to stay focused and empowered in the present moment. Sporting the wounds of the past often offers us the attention we crave and helps us justify our lack of willingness to take responsibility for our present experience.

Very little is gained on the spiritual path as a result of these excursions into yesterday or tomorrow. The projected dramas of past or future are distractions that take us away from the real challenge of being present here and now.

It is important to watch how our minds continue to grasp for external answers to our problems and how fascinated we get in the imagery of change. What does not change is far less interesting to us. We don't like being told "there's nothing out there to get!" When the guru tells us to go home and follow our breath, we are disappointed. We had hoped that s/he would send us on another retreat, another crusade or another mission of mercy.

There are enough windy, circuitous roads out there to keep us traveling for a long time. There are enough detours on the spiritual path to keep us spinning our wheels ad infinitum. After taking enough of them, we realize that none of them are going anywhere in particular. They all eventually bring us back to the place where we started.

We have taken enough of these useless journeys. The time has come to anchor in the heart. We don't have to be concerned about what happened in the past or what will happen in the future. We don't need any more stories to put us to sleep.

Dropping our Stories

Our stories of the past reinforce our fears and justify our rituals of self-protection. Whenever we connect with what we want, we also connect with all the reasons why we can't have it. "I want to leave my job, but I can't....I want to commit to this relationship, but I can't." On and on it goes.... the perpetual "Catch 22." We want to bring new energy into our lives and hold onto our old habits at the same time. We want change, but we are afraid of it.

In some ways, we prefer our pain just the way it is because it is a known quantity. We think that if we make a change in our lives, things could get worse. The pain could be greater. We prefer a known pain to an unknown pain, a familiar suffering to an unfamiliar one.

Our egos are deeply committed to the status quo of our lives, because it is predictable. That's why the spiritual adult's heroic plans for the transformation of our lives are inevitably undermined by the fears of the wounded child, who doesn't think s/he is lovable, and therefore cannot have a vision of a life without pain. To the wounded kid within, any promise of release from pain is a trick that entices us to let our defenses down and become vulnerable to attack.

So our fears keep us closed to the possibility of meaningful change in our lives. What we say we want is not what we really want. The spiritual adult and the wounded child are at odds, and, when that happens, the wounded child always wins. Unfortunately, that does not lead to happiness for either adult or child. It leads only to the prolongation of our familiar, internalized suffering and pain.

Into this duplicitous environment of the psyche at war with itself then come a variety of professional fixers: psychiatrists, counselors, preachers, self-help gurus. Each claims to have the answer, but each solution offered and taken just compounds the problem. When we think there is something wrong with us, we reinforce our unworthiness. When we try to fix ourselves, we reinforce our belief that something in us is broken.

Professional fixers believe our stories of brokenness and try to heal us. They reinforce our stories. If our story isn't juicy enough story, they help us make it more juicy. It's all about high drama, about sin and salvation. It never occurs to them or to us that maybe nothing is broken, that maybe there is nothing in us that needs to be fixed. It never occurs to them or to us that the only dysfunctional aspect of our situation is our belief that something is broken, our belief that we will never get what we want.

The external problems we perceive in our lives are projections of the internal conflict: "I want but I cannot have." If we would allow ourselves to have what we want, or if we would stop wanting it because we know we can't have it, this conflict would cease. Having what we want or accepting that we can't have it ends our conflict. In the process, it ends our story.

If we have what we want or if we've made our peace with not having it, we have no story. There's no drama of seeking. To keep the drama of seeking going, you cannot find what you are seeking. Finding love, happiness, joy, and so forth ends the story. "And they lived happily ever after...." Story over. Drama complete. Now, what's next?

The truth is we're not ready to give up our dramas. Our story has become part of our identity. Our pain is part of our personality. We do not know who we are without it. Letting our drama go means letting the past dissolve right here, right now.

If we can do that, it doesn't matter what happened in the past. It has no power. It doesn't exist any more. We are writing on a clean slate.

That means that right now we are totally responsible for what we choose. There are no more excuses. We can't blame what happens on the past or on our karma, because there is no more past, no more karma.

When we no longer interpret our lives based on what happened yesterday or last year, what happens is neutral. It is what it is. There is no charge on it.

The freedom to be fully present and responsible right now is awesome. Very few people want it. Most people want to wear their past like a noose around their necks. They insist on carrying their cross and wearing their crown of thorns. That way if they get crucified, they can say "I told you this would happen." Another self-fulfilling prophecy!

We stay in the drama because we love it. We keep dragging our karma with us because we are attached to it. And so we have to heal all the make-believe wounds we think that we have. It doesn't matter that those wounds are not real. They are real enough to us.

And so the drama continues. Seek but do not find. I want, but I can't have. I want to be free, but I want my security too.

You can't tell a person who is in prison getting three meals a day that freedom is its own security. S/he wants those three meals a day no matter what. Then s/he will talk about freedom.

When you are attached to what you already have, how can you bring in anything new in? To bring in something new, something fresh, something unpredictable, you must surrender something old, stale and habitual.

If you want the creative to manifest within you, you must surrender all that is not creative. Then in the space made by that surrender, creativity rushes in. If the cup is full of old, cold tea, you cannot pour new, hot tea into it. First you have to empty the cup. Then you can fill it.

If you want to give up your drama, first find out what your investment is in it. What is your pay-off for not finding, not healing, not living happily ever after?

And then be honest. If you don't want to move through your pain, tell the truth. Say "I'm not ready to move through my pain yet." Don't say "I wish I could be done with my pain, but I can't be." That is a lie. You could be done with it, but you don't choose to be. Perhaps you enjoy the attention you get being a victim.

Most people who claim to be on the spiritual path

are just spinning their wheels. They are always saying "yes, but..." They are always making excuses. For the person who has learned to accept responsibility, there are no excuses. S/he knows it all belongs to him or her. It has nothing to do with anyone else.

When s/he is not ready s/he says "I am not ready." When s/he is ready, s/he does not have to make any promises. For actions flow from readiness, and actions always speak louder than words.

Freedom and Commitment

If the truth is that we can do anything that we want, then there are no more excuses. If we are not doing what we want, then we must not want it enough. Or perhaps it is what we think we should want. Maybe we are trying to live someone else's dream, instead of our own.

You can be sure that your dream doesn't look like anyone else's. It is unique to you. When you compare yourself to others, you can't act in an authentic way.

If you are not committed to your goal, you must question it. Being free to pursue your goal means nothing if you are not committed to it. If you don't want to do something, if you are not willing to put the full force of your being behind it, then it isn't going to happen. But that's not because there's anything out there stopping you from meeting your goal. It's because it's not what you really want.

People are ineffective for two reasons. Either they don't know what they want or they don't believe in it.

When you know what you want and you believe in it, nothing can stop you from bringing that into your life. Of course, when you bring it in, it might look a little different than you expected it to. Your ego might object to it. But that's a different problem.

Your job is not to know how manifestation is going to happen or what it is going to look like. Your job is to get clear on what you want and be totally committed to it. Then, however it happens and however it looks, you better accept it. Because if you do not accept and celebrate the fruit of your labors, you will disempower yourself. When you find fault with your experience, you make it difficult if not impossible for grace to happen in your life.

Everybody wants a formula for manifestation, but few want to practice the formula. The formula's easy. The practice is what challenges.

A Formula for Creation

1. First, get clear on what you want. Unless you want something, heart and soul, you will have difficulty creating it. Take as long as you need to get clear. It might take a day, a month, a year, a lifetime. If you try to create without knowing what you want, you will waste time and energy. You will also be training yourself to be a failure. Don't jump the gun or ask for something you're not sure that you want.

2. Believe in what you want and move toward it steadily, no matter how implausible it seems or how many obstacles seem to be in your way. Without your total commitment, your goal cannot be realized. Do not waver in your commitment until what you want has manifested in your life.

3. When you create what you want, celebrate it. Be grateful for it. Give up your pictures of the way you thought it would be. Drop your expectations. Embrace it just the way it is. Work with it. Use it. Love it and keep on loving it.

Your job is to be clear about the goal, committed to it, and grateful for its accomplishment in your life. You don't have to know "how" the goal is going to be realized in your life. Just do the best you can.

Follow any strategy that feels right to you.

Remember, it is not the strategy that brings you toward your goal, but your desire to reach it and your commitment to accomplish it. When these factors are in place, the strategy you need will make itself known to you. When you know "what" you want and "why" you want it, "when, where and how" will be revealed to you.

All creation is really co-creation. You determine what you want, commit to it, and move toward it, and the opportunities you need to realize your goal come your way. To be sure, you must keep your eyes open. You must keep surrendering your expectations and be willing to see the opportunities that arise, but you do not have to make them happen. They happen all by themselves.

One of the great "Ahahs" on the spiritual path is the recognition that you don't have to make your life happen. It happens by itself.

When you know what you want, what you need to realize it is spontaneously offered by the universe. This is what effortlessness and non-striving teach us. We don't have to work to make things happen. We don't have to sacrifice, beg, borrow or steal. We just have to be clear and committed.

Of course, there is one more important thing. We

must believe that we are worthy of having what we want. If we don't believe that we are worthy, it doesn't matter how good our process is. We will find a way to undermine it. We won't want it enough. We won't be committed enough to it.

We struggle when we don't feel worthy. We oppose our own goals. As long as this inner block is there, we cannot realize our dreams or our goals.

In the garden, Adam and Eve are innocent. They feel worthy of God's love. As soon as they cease to feel worthy, they are banished from the garden. What used to be easy becomes hard. Play becomes work. Fulfillment becomes sacrifice.

It is impossible to create without God. When your will is separate from the divine Will, creation cannot happen. When you do not feel worthy of God's love, you cannot find love in the world. If you are afraid or ashamed, find a way to hold the fear and the shame with compassion, so that you can release them gently into the arms of love.

God does not want you to struggle. God does not want you to beat yourself. God just asks you to be humble. S/he wants you to know that you can't create successfully from your limited ego consciousness.

"Know thyself and to thine own self be true." That

is your part. The rest belongs to God. Surrender the how. You cannot know.

The desire to know takes you out of the garden. It takes you out of relationship with God.

To trust God means to trust the deepest part of your being. It means to trust in your unlimited, resourceful Self. No, not the part that needs to sit down and figure everything out. Not the part that needs guarantees. That part cannot be trusted, nor can it trust. It is and will always be insecure, because it does not know that it is loved.

But the part of you that knows it is loved, and feels worthy of that love, that you can trust. That is the link between you and God. As you rest in that certainty, what you need in your life is created gracefully. As you rely more on God within you and less on your limited self which does not feel loved, your struggle is diminished. Your sacrifice comes to an end.

Remember, the path out of the garden leads inevitably to Golgotha. In the end, the world will endeavor to take from you everything except what you have been willing to give to yourself.

Don't take the journey to the cross. It is a useless and unnecessary one. If you have not learned that from my life, learn it now.

Even Jesus can be crucified. No man can take on the world's pain and survive. It is not by taking on your pain that I become free, but by showing you how to leave your own pain behind.

The journey of awakening goes from unconscious innocence to the fall from grace, from guilt to responsibility to self-forgiveness. Innocence is not soiled by experience but redeemed in it and by it, as Blake knew. The one who insists on knowing will be crucified by his own lack of faith, but he will learn to trust in the bargain. When Adam returns to the garden, he will be naked once again, but he won't be tempted to trade his salvation for the promise of external fulfillment.

That we can know the truth only by being it initiates the journey of becoming and concludes it. In the end, we land where we began, in the garden, where each of us is Adam and Eve, serpent and redeemer.

Creating Heaven on Earth

The true price of freedom is not suffering, but responsibility. Instead of trying to make someone else responsible for your mistakes, you acknowledge and learn from them. You change the way you think and act. You begin to clean up the mess you made.

As you do, the garden begins to bloom again. You plant new flowers and trees, water the soil and pull up the weeds. You become responsible for your creations and they thrive. What you reap at harvest time depends on what you sow each day.

That is the life you chose when you came into this embodiment. Those are the laws you must work with. You must live with your mistakes until you correct them. And unless you learn to forgive the past and create with greater foresight and responsibility, you will experience some version of hell on earth.

This planet is a learning laboratory that helps you develop the self confidence and sensitivity to others that you need to create the conditions that are best for the common good. At this time, your garden is parched and overgrown by weeds. It has not been tended kindly or responsibly. Nobody else can tend it for you.

Every thought you have, every emotion you indulge, every action you take weighs in. So consider these well. Ask yourself how they will impact others and yourself. Do not forge ahead blindly driven by your doubt, your anger, and your fear. You cannot afford to create out of that place anymore. Earth has given you notice. Water and wind have risen up and spoken to you in your dreams. Fire has appeared to you as it did to Moses. There are no secrets here.

To many of you, it seems that life is speeding up. All the more reason why you must slow down. How else can you inhabit the present moment? You can't address all that has happened in the past. You can only address what is happening now.

It is time for you to live each day as though it were your last, to live each moment as though it were the only moment you have. If you can do that, you will be a good gardener. You will have the peace of mind and the silence of heart that result from responsible creation.

When you return to the garden, you are different from the way you were when you left. You left hell-bent on expressing your own creativity at any cost. You return humble and sensitive to the needs of all.

You return not as just as created but also as creator, not just as son of man, but also as son of God. From Adam to Christ, you come full circle.

Trusting the Christ Within

When you act out of fear, you don't solve any problems. You just add to the imbalance and the hysteria. Don't act out of fear. Let the fear come up.

Ride it as a wave and return to your center. Then it will be time to act.

Realize that you have just the amount of time that you need to complete your journey. So don't rush. But don't hesitate either. Proceed forward with faith, confidence, and enthusiasm. Take no thought for yesterday or tomorrow. What you say and do today will be enough.

Move in the direction of your greatest joy. Choose something to do that will express your love, your gratitude, your appreciation.

Don't beat yourself because you suffered in the past. Forgive the past and move on.

Do what you have always wanted to do. If nobody wants to pay you to do it, do it for free. If nobody encourages you, redouble your efforts. Do not withhold your gift. The salvation of the world depends on all people expressing the gifts they have.

Don't worry about the future. You are the one creating it. Don't tie it down to the past. Release it to do its work. Have faith. Don't be attached to the results. Trust.

The one you are trusting is God incarnate, the Christ him or herself. How can you fear the future when Christ is with you. Put your trust in that One.

Part Three
The Practice

Opening to Jesus

If you resonate with the words you are reading, it may be that you are ready to embrace the teachings of Jesus as your spiritual path. Do be aware, though, that you cannot embrace these teachings without also embracing the teacher.

While Jesus is not here in a body, he is very much present and available to you. To be in communion with him requires simply a willingness and openness on your part.

You can open to Jesus as a teacher regardless of your religious background. You don't have to be a Christian. Open minded Jews find it easier to connect with Jesus than some Christians do because they have an easier time accepting him as a teacher and an equal. Remember, it is easier to have a relationship with an equal than with someone you place on a pedestal.

But the truth is that Jesus cares not about your dogmas, be they Christian or Buddhist, Hindu, Jewish or Muslim. He cares only about your willingness to remember the truth of who you are.

You develop a relationship with Jesus as you enter into dialogue with him, seek his guidance, and understand and practice his teachings. But how do you take the first step and initiate the dialogue?

Acknowledge Your Teacher

I do not know why this is so important, but I can tell you that my relationship with Jesus did not come into fullness until I acknowledged him as he had asked me to do. The fact is that I could not accept his teaching and deny him. At a minimum, I had to acknowledge him as the author of the teaching. If I liked the teaching, I needed to accept the teacher.

This acknowledgment enabled Jesus to move from abstract concept to real presence in my life. It initiated a series of dreams and inner dialogues. Now, I acknowledge Jesus on a regular basis, privately and publicly. He is the Friend, my companion on the spiritual path. When things become difficult, it is his guidance I seek.

While your experience will not look like mine, I know that the issue of acknowledgement will be important. When you talk to someone, you call that person by name. You address that person in a unique manner that is different from the way you would approach someone else.

As I have worked with people in opening to the

Christ consciousness in their hearts, I have seen a major energetic movement happen when people address Jesus specifically. Often, this is the first time they experience energy in their hearts. Once you have felt his presence energetically, it is hard to pretend that he not there when you address him.

Going into the Silence

Once or twice each day, for at least ten or fifteen minutes, make time to go into the silence. Put aside what preoccupies you, be still, and listen. You might find it helpful to do some yoga or deep breathing first to relax your body and calm your mind.

Sit or lie down in a comfortable position and just relax into the silence. As thoughts or feelings come up, just be aware of them and accept them. In the space between your thoughts, there will be a deep peace and stillness. Dwell there. Be completely alert and present there.

Sometimes when you rest in the silence, you may hear a voice, see an image, or have some insight that has nothing to do with any of your everyday thoughts. When this happens, you feel an inner peace and rightness about what you have heard, seen or understood. That is a sign that you have heard your guidance. Guidance comes from the place in you which is connected to God. Receive it gratefully. Learn to trust it and act on it. The more you do, the easier it will be for you to hear the truth as it unfolds within your consciousness.

By going into the silence on a regular basis, you will be doing what Jesus did as he developed a relationship with the indwelling God. The more you trust that relationship, the more it can begin to guide your actions in the world, bringing you step by step in line with your life purpose.

A Mantra that Works

Even in the course of your daily life, you can be doing spiritual practice. Whenever you find yourself getting confused, anxious, fearful, angry, etc., ask yourself "Am I loving myself right now?" This question helps you understand that beneath all thoughts and behaviors of separation lies the refusal to be gentle and loving toward ourselves.

Even if your anger or upset feelings are directed toward someone else, you aren't being loving toward yourself. Indeed, the only way that you can be angry at anyone else is to forget to love yourself. When you are loving yourself, it is not possible to be angry at anyone else.

The mantra "Am I loving myself right now?" reminds you of your only responsibility while here in this embodiment: to love and take care of yourself. When love is established in your heart, it flows automatically to others.

This is anything but a selfish practice. It is a practice that takes you back to your heart, where love originates.

When you see that you aren't being loving toward yourself, you know what you need to do to return to peace. If you are having an argument with someone, you need to stop and say: "Excuse me, but I just realized that I'm not being loving either toward myself or toward you right now. I need to have some time to attune to love. Otherwise, I know I'll say things that I don't mean. Can we have a little break and come back to this conversation later?"

When you know that you are not being loving, you need to stop and find a way to connect with love. Take a walk, do some deep breathing. Be aware of the judgments you are carrying about others and how they reflect your judgment about aspects of yourself you have trouble accepting. Work on accepting yourself right now in this moment. If there is a disagreement with someone, work on accepting the disagreement. Let this moment be okay just the way it is. It doesn't have to be perfect to be acceptable. Be aware that your inability to accept this moment extends it indefinitely. Most feelings shift when you accept them. Lack of acceptance just prolongs your pain.

If you are very angry, you may not be ready to have this conversation with yourself. First, you might need to run around the block, go to a deserted beach and yell, or hit a pillow. Don't take your anger out on someone else. That will just create more pain for you. Find a harmless way to express your anger. Then look at how your anger crucifies you and holds you hostage to your pain. It may be provoked by someone else, but it is never anyone else's responsibility.

Integrating the Dark Side

In the end, even anger must be accepted and forgiven. When you know anger is about you, not about someone else, you know that the hardest thing is to forgive yourself. When you are angry, the hidden dark side comes into plain view. It isn't easy to accept this dark side. It isn't easy to see the pain and the cry for love behind it. But this is how you

heal. You become aware of the dark, disenfranchised aspects of self and bring them into conscious
awareness. You redeem them. You bring your darkness to the light.

It is not an easy process, this synergy of dark and
light within your own soul, but it is a necessary one.
It is part of the birth of spirit in your life. It is the way
that man becomes God, that the Fall from grace
turns, as it hits the existential floor of being, and
becomes the Ascension back to the divine.

You must redeem the parts of yourself you have
abandoned or betrayed. If you have cut off your
sexuality, you must reclaim it. If you have neglected
your creativity or repressed your power, you must
find a way to accept and express these important
aspects of self.

Most of us project what we dislike or are afraid of
in ourselves onto others. If we are afraid of our
power, we project it onto some powerful, charis-
matic figure through whom we try to live. When
that person takes advantage of us or betrays us, we
feel angry. We may even seek revenge. This takes us
away from our healing and understanding into
interactive conflict, in which our pain and feelings of
powerlessness only deepen.

This whole event is impersonal. The person to

whom we gave our power away could have been anyone who was compensating for feelings of inferiority by acting self-assured and over-confident. An unconscious match took place, helping both of us come to grips with our inability to embrace our own authentic power.

We experience conflict in relationship because others mirror back to us what we don't want to see in ourselves. If we insist on making the other person the problem, we can't learn our own lessons. That is why we must learn to view our relationships as learning laboratories that unmask our self-deceptions and help us see our doubt, fear, and guilt in the plain light of day.

Relationship as a Spiritual Path

It is a difficult but important fact that very few of us experience happiness in our relationships. This is the case primarily because we expect our relationships to enhance and improve our lives. We think we can be happier with someone else than we can be with ourselves.

If you think about it, this expectation is absurd! How could we be happier with someone else than we are with ourselves? The truth is that we can be only as happy with another person as we can be with ourselves. Our capacity to enjoy our relationship with another depends on our capacity to enjoy our relationship with ourselves. Why would it be otherwise?

So if we want to use our relationship as a path for spiritual understanding and growth, the first thing we must give up is the romantic fantasy that the other person can be the source of our happiness. We are the source of our happiness. If we are happy, being with our partner can be an extension of our happiness. But, if we are not happy, being with our partner will only exacerbate our unhappiness. In other words, being in relationship with another is just as challenging, if not more challenging than being alone.

So we need to be clear about that. Our decision to enter into partnership should not be based on a desire to avoid looking at self, but on a willingness to intensify that process. We cannot escape ourselves by moving into relationship. Quite the opposite. Being in relationship simply requires us to face ourselves more deeply.

In our own spiritual practice, we learn to take others off the hook and take responsibility for what we think, feel and experience. Others may trigger our feelings — positive or negative — but they are not responsible for how we feel. We are responsible for every thought that we think and every feeling that we have.

To be sure, taking responsibility for our experience in each moment is no easy task, even when we live alone. But when we live with someone else, the level of difficulty is greatly increased. When we live with someone, we are likely to be triggered more often. And so we will have to take responsibility for our thoughts and feelings more often.

Also, when we live with someone, we are likely to trigger their unhealed wounds. And if our partners are not skilled at taking responsibility for how they think and feel, they may tend to blame us when their doubts and fears rise to the surface. We need to be careful not to take inappropriate responsibility for our partner's pain and unhappiness.

Our relationships give us plenty of practice taking responsibility for our experience (not projecting) and denying responsibility for how another person thinks or feels (not being a target for our partner's projections). If we can learn from the constant practice our relationship provides, we can accelerate our spiritual growth and understanding. In the process, our relationship can become a sacred one.

In a sacred relationship, we take responsibility for meeting our own needs. This includes asking our partner for what we want, and accepting our partner's honest response. When our partner is able to be responsive to what we want, we express our appreciation. When our partner is not able to respond, we accept that and find ways to meet our needs that are not hurtful to our partner or damaging to our relationship.

When our relationship is sacred, we aren't dependent on or dishonest with one another. We tell the truth, share what we can, and support each other in finding channels for creative self-expression and service. We don't want to hold each other back, nor do we want to push each other away.

Transcending Boundaries

A spiritual relationship is built on a strong sense of boundaries. We know where our responsibility is and isn't. But such a relationship also leads to a deepening trust in which the boundaries between self and other dissolve in unconditional love and service.

For example, John may see that Jessica is feeling sad and discouraged when he decides not to go to dinner at her parent's house. He knows that he is not responsible for how Jessica feels, that he can keep his heart open to Jessica and still decide to stay home and finish correcting his students' papers.

John is clear that he is okay. He's also clear that Jessica is okay. He knows that she will get over her sadness when she is ready. But he feels compassion for Jessica. He knows what it is like when he wants Jessica to do something with him and she decides she doesn't want to. It doesn't feel good.

So John comes over and puts his arms around Jessica and says: "Maybe I could join you and your parents for desert after I finish correcting these papers. Would you like that?" And that little gesture helps Jessica to feel loved and appreciated.

Now, is John responsible for Jessica feeling loved and appreciated? Not at all. It's not his responsibility. If he makes it his responsibility, he will become enmeshed and co-dependent with Jessica. He is not responsible for Jessica's happiness nor does he want to be. But he feels compassion for her. So he decides of his own free will to do something that he thinks may be pleasing to her. No one is coercing him to do this. Jessica does not expect it. It is not part of a pattern in which John is always trying to please Jessica and, as a result, is not taking care of himself.

John does not violate himself. He doesn't sacrifice

something that is important to him. He knows that he can make this gesture without being attached to whether or not Jessica responds to it, without expecting anything from Jessica in return. It is simply a gesture of compassion made spontaneously in the moment.

When boundaries have been respected in a relationship, it is possible to go beyond them. When we feel honored by our partner, it is easy for us to act in a kind and unselfish manner toward him or her. There is no sacrifice or self-denial in this. Rather, there is an expansion of our love, in which we learn to care as deeply for the happiness of the other as we do for our own happiness.

No, we don't become responsible for our partner's happiness. That's codependency and a lack of appropriate boundaries. Instead, we hold our partner's happiness as equal to our own. Our love for ourselves and our love for our partner become inseparable. The boundaries of self and other are gently and profoundly erased. Lover and beloved join in eternal embrace.

There can be no sacrifice or compulsion in our surrender, or it is not surrender, but capitulation. We cannot go beyond self if we do not know who we are or who the other is. But when we know the truth about self and other, when we experience our essential and complete equality with another person, the lines of separation fade into oblivion. Now only Christ is present, in ourselves and in the other. This is the One Self, the Friend Eternal, the compassionate One Him or Herself.

Unselfish Actions

When we have given birth to Christ in a single relationship with another human being, we have taken the first step into the circle of grace. Having experienced what it is like to hold one person's happiness equally with our own, we can learn to do this in other relationships.

We can practice doing unselfish acts for others without expecting anything in return. And we can experience the joy that comes from giving without strings attached.

When we give without thought of return, the law of grace manifests through us. We become the vehicle through which God's love expresses in this world.

Obviously, we cannot give unconditionally to others unless we are feeling loved ourselves. True giving is an overflowing of our love. We don't feel that we are being depleted when we give in this way. In fact, we feel energized, because the love we give away always returns to us through the gratitude of others who share with us how we have touched their lives.

Seeing the innocence and the beauty in others and letting them know that we see it is the greatest gift that we can give. When we can see that beauty and innocence not just in those who treat us well, but also in those who misunderstand or attack us, then we know that we are anchored in the Christ consciousness of unconditional love.

In order to do this, we must be so strongly convinced that we are loved and lovable that we can see all attack on us as error or illusion. We look past this error and see the person behind it who is feeling fearful and unloved. We feel compassion for his or her pain. We know the attack on us comes out of that pain, that desperation. And we know that only our love can touch that pain and transform it.

We don't withhold our love from those who need it, even when they seem to be asking for it in offensive ways. We reach down to the place in us that knows that love is everpresent and eternal no matter what seems to be happening. And we find a way to respond in a caring way to the person striking out against us.

The teachings of Jesus are very clear on this point. Our responsibility is not just to love the people we like and admire. We are asked to love our enemies too. In the end, there is no one who is unworthy of our love.

This is a simple, but uncompromising teaching. We start practicing it by bringing each person we meet into our acceptance and love. We recognize when we are being challenged and dig down to find that ever-deepening Source of love within us. Those who challenge us are in this sense our greatest teachers. They push us to the limit, forcing us to move through our own walls of fear and judgment.

As we follow the path laid out by Jesus, we look less and less to see how we are being treated, and more and more to see how we are treating others. We learn to be loving toward others even when they are not being loving toward us. We don't focus on their words and actions. We focus on our own.

We know that we can offer others either our fear or our love. Our responsibility is to move through our fears into the consciousness of unshakable love. When people respond to us in an aggressive way, our fears are often triggered and we are given an opportunity to move consciously through them. As we do, we put them behind us, transcending reactive emotions so that we can respond in a caring way.

There is no greater learning on the spiritual path than this. When we learn to respond to the fears of others in a loving way, we can be sure that our own fears rest in the most compassionate embrace. We are no longer emotionally reactive or ambivalent, but patient and steady, knowing that only love is real. Everything else is illusion.

Ministering/Mentoring

When the truth is known and embodied, it can easily be understood. Each person who becomes authentic and compassionate becomes a model for others. That person may be a teacher, a family friend or relative, a business person, a big brother or sister. It is not what s/he does or says that is so important. It is how s/he does it or says. A true mentor/minister expresses caring and love in his or her words and deeds.

Such people are magnetic and compelling, not necessarily because they have achieved important things in the world, but because they care and you can feel it. Love has risen up in them and it overflows them, anointing all who come their way.

When you learn to love yourself, you cannot help loving others. It is not hard to do. It's automatic.

We think that Jesus is special because he loved so many people. But really he is one among many who moved into the lap of love and became its perpetual minister. When you love, there is no limit on that love. It constantly recycles, flowing in and out of the heart. Like waves breaking and receding on a beach, the tides of love are steady and dependable. They touch every shoreline with their blessing.

Love is not something we do. Love is who we are. We are the embodiment of love in this moment. Nothing less.

But all this begins in our own hearts. It begins with our willingness to love and accept ourselves. That is where Christ is born.

Once born, He cannot be contained. There is no place where He cannot go. There is no place where His love cannot reach.

Wherever you go, Christ goes with you. He moves with your legs, reaches with your hands, speaks with your voice, and sees with your eyes.

Because of you, He is everywhere. Without you, He would be invisible. Is that not why you too must become a witness, a mentor, a minister of the love that abides in you and in all beings? No, not to preach or proselytize, but to listen, to comfort, to care. In your silence, His presence is felt; in your acceptance, His compassion is experienced; in your smile, His delight is made manifest.

The love that expresses through you is the Christ Presence Itself, the human vehicle ablaze with the divine light, the very embodiment of God's love. Jesus was and is the Christ, but He is not the only one.

We are the second coming, you and I. We are the ones who have been asked to open our hearts, our minds and our arms so that the love of God can be experienced in this embodiment.

When Jesus heard the call, he answered it. Now we hear it too. And we answer it by following the teaching which he gave to us then and continues to give to us now: "whatever is not loving must be forgiven; and what is forgiven becomes love's patient blessing on an imperfect world.

Not Fixing Others

Many times I have been told by my teacher that no one needs to be fixed. As soon as I think anyone (including me) needs to be fixed, I am already buying into scarcity thinking. And nothing ever gets fixed through scarcity thinking.

It's a paradox. If I think it needs to be fixed, then fixing it will be impossible. If I realize that it can't be fixed, then it isn't broken. The key in this sentence is the word "I." What I think determines the drama, or lack of it.

The question always is: "Am I willing to accept this situation the way it is?" If I am, then I can learn from it and move on. If I'm not, then I will prod it, poke it, prolong it, and generally make it much worse than it seemed to begin with.

Because we want things to be perfect, we are always trying to change our experience. By insisting on perfection, we experience imperfection. Only when we accept things just as they are do we experience the inherent perfection of all things.

One of the greatest of the Christ Mind practices is that of acceptance. Yet how many of us find it easy to accept life as it unfolds?

Most of us try to practice acceptance, but instead we see that we are constantly finding fault with our experience. When we see that, we can choose to beat ourselves up or we can accept the fact that we are finding fault. If we beat ourselves up, we will reinforce our lack of acceptance. This becomes a vicious cycle in which find ourselves continually inadequate.

So we learn to be aware of what's happening

without judging it. We observe: "I am trying to be accepting, but I see I have a lot of judgments about what's going on. I'm also aware that I feel bad about having these judgments. It doesn't seem very spiritual. I see that I am sitting here judging my judgments. That's what's going on. And it's okay. It's not a problem. It's just what's happening."

When we say the last four sentences, we're beginning to speak the language of acceptance. This takes the pressure off. Now it's okay for things to be imperfect or unfinished. Now I can be judging and not feeling like a failure. Now I can be compassionate with myself, others, and the situation at hand.

When acceptance happens, we look at things differently. The problems we perceive when we are finding fault with our lives often disappear when we can be okay with what is happening. Accepting is like taking a deep breath and relaxing. The more we accept, the more we deepen in our feelings of peace and well-being.

When we are peaceful, we don't need to fix anyone or anything. If something needs to change, the necessary change will happen by itself. It doesn't need to be forced. It doesn't take great effort or manipulation.

When we are upset or agitated, we ready to fix

our problems and everyone else's problems. We get contracted. We exude fear or anger. We tense up, forget to breathe, and get ready to attack or retreat. We act as though we are going into battle, except that the battle is taking place only in our own minds.

We're not going to stop this from happening. We're going to experience anxiety, frustration, fight or flight. The question is not "How can we avoid getting upset?" but "How will we handle things when we get upset?" Will agitation lead to panic? Will fear lead to paranoia? Will we turn purple because we don't remember to breathe? Or will we see that we are getting upset and remember to breathe, relax, accept the situation just as it is.

Clearly, this is a spiritual practice. When we want to jump in and fix somebody, we need to become aware of our own fear, our own agitation. We need to remember that acting from that place of fear only exacerbates the situation. We need to catch the judgment before we speak it and hold it compassionately within our own awareness.

We can't always stop things from happening in a certain way, but we can stop reacting to them out of fear. We can slow down, pause, listen, breathe, come back into our hearts.

Accepting/not fixing doesn't happen overnight. It is a process. It doesn't ask us to make things better. It simply asks us not to make things worse.

When we refuse to fix, we eliminate the impact of our judgments and interpretations on the events and circumstances of our life. And life always unfolds better when we get out of the way.

Listening Without Feedback

Sometimes we try to fix others in subtle ways. We appear to be listening to our friends when they talk to us, but we often listen with our own filters. In our own minds, we are agreeing or disagreeing with them, seeing what they are saying in the context of our own life and our own beliefs. Clearly, we are not listening unconditionally, neutrally, without having an opinion. And so, in a certain way, we aren't really listening at all.

When our friends confide in us, we often think that this is an invitation to us to analyze their situation or give advice. We then jump in with all our own issues and judgments. It is not surprising that others may not feel that they have been heard by us.

One of the key Christ Mind practices is to listen without judgment to what people are saying and to refrain from offering any judgment, or interpretation about it. If people ask for feedback, we tell them that we think we understand what they are saying and we feedback what we have heard as accurately as possible. Usually when we do this, people are pleasantly surprised. "Wow," they often say, "You really heard me."

Being really heard is a rare event. How many times have we felt really heard? How many times have we listened to others unconditionally without trying to solve their problems?

When we give advice to others, we get involved in their problems. You would think we would realize that we have enough challenges in our lives; we don't need to take on other people's problems. But we do, because by taking on their problems, we try to work out our own. We project our dreams and fears onto other people's dramas. We watch soap operas for the same reason.

Since most of us are not very successful in solving our own problems, it isn't very likely that we will be able to help other people work out their issues. Moreover, we don't really understand the context of another person's life. So even those solutions that worked for us are not necessarily going to be relevant to someone else.

When we try to fix or give advice to others, we are not being kind or generous. Rather, we are attacking them. If we want to be kind to others, we need to accept them the way they are and stop trying to judge, analyze, interpret, or change their lives.

We do this by realizing that they are okay just as they are in this moment. We hold the consciousness of their present perfection. If they want to share their problems with us, we listen with compassion, but we don't offer opinions or solutions. We let them know that we have heard them. We might even share a time in our own lives when we were feeling a similar way, but we don't pretend that our situation is the same as theirs or that what worked for us would work for them. Instead, we encourage them to stay in their own process and find their own guidance. We feel confident that all the answers are within them, just as they are within all of us.

When we trust others to find their own answers, we treat them as spiritual equals. We don't pretend to know something they don't know. We don't want them to be dependent on us. We grant people both respect and freedom. We trust the truth within them to light their way. That is love in action. That is the kind of unconditional love Jesus asked us to offer one another.

Not fixing others means that we don't take inappropriate responsibility for their lives. That gives us the time and energy we need to take appropriate responsibility for our own lives. By taking good care of ourselves on all levels — physically, emotionally, mentally, and spiritually — we are able to respond to others in the most compassionate, patient, and caring way. By contrast, if we neglect our responsibilities to ourselves and try to take responsibility for others, we get depleted energetically. Then we aren't in a position to be helpful to anyone.

It is a revelation to some of us to know that we are not here to rescue others from their pain, but merely to walk through our own. No one else can do that for us. It is our essential responsibility and will be throughout this embodiment. Even when we join our life with another person's life, this responsibility stays with us. Whenever we lose sight of it, or try to give it to someone else, we inevitably pay the price.

The Affinity Process

In order to help people develop skillfulness in listening, accepting, and not fixing, the *Affinity Process* was developed. The goal of the Process is to hold a space of unconditional love and acceptance for each member of the group. Most groups have eight to ten members and meet once per week for at least eight weeks. A set of guidelines helps members to keep the group space loving, safe, and compassionate.

Using the guidelines, members become aware of just how many judgments they are holding about others in the group and, ultimately, about themselves. They learn to hold these judgments compassionately in awareness and come back into their hearts where they can be present for others and listen deeply.

Affinity Group members also have the opportunity to talk about any matter which is heavy on their hearts and to be listened to without judgment by the other members. Since the guidelines rule out any kind of analyzing or fixing, members get to experience what it is like to confess something important and to have that held in great acceptance, gentleness, and compassion by the group. Often, in the light of that compassionate acceptance, the speaker will realize that the conflict or problem just dissolves, or something shifts inside that enables him or her to hold that problem in a lighter, less self-condemning way.

When problems are given into a state of consciousness which sees what is as perfect, there is nothing that supports the problem. Without support, the problem ceases to be. It remains a problem only if the person offering it up holds onto it. That happens when the person speaking refuses to enter into the consciousness of unconditional love which permeates the group. While that happens once and a while, it is rare. Separation is a temporary state and, when love is present, most people will tend to breathe, let go and surrender into it.

There is a state of consciousness in which fear dissolves, problems cannot exist and only love is present. Using the guidelines of the *Affinity Process*, that state can be experienced, not just in the group, but at home. Affinity group members report that they are able to use their newfound skills in their relationships with spouses, children, parents, friends, bosses, and co-workers. When the guidelines are practiced, even by just one person, the conditions for conflict are dissolved.

For several years, Jesus has emphasized the daily practice of the Christ Mind principles. "You already know what you need to do. You just need to do it." We have all the head knowledge we need to walk the spiritual path, but we don't practice it. We don't integrate our knowledge into our daily lives. The *Affinity Process* gives us a concrete practice that we can do once a week with a small group of people. By meeting once per week, it fulfills our commitment to observe the Sabbath: to set aside a time each week that is reserved just for the purpose of remembering God.

Affinity Group practice is a contemporary marriage of the rituals of confession and communion. It offers each person an opportunity to express any fear, anxiety, shame or guilt which prevents him or her from seeing his innocence or that of any other person. It purifies our hearts and minds, and restores our connection to the unconditional love of God. It also affirms our connection to our teacher by providing us with a hands-on practice of non-judgment, acceptance, and forgiveness.

More than any other practice, the Affinity Group practice helps us to experience what it is like to live in Christ consciousness. At first, it may be for just a few minutes during a two hour meeting. But gradually, as we learn to hold the space, we often experience uninterrupted, ecstatic acceptance for a whole session.

Our weekly practice anchors these skills in our daily life. We don't stop practicing when we go home. We just change classrooms. More and more, we bring the practice of non-judgment and acceptance into our moment to moment experience. And, as we do, peace and ecstasy become a way of life.

Community Service

When members complete the eight week *Affinity Process*, they are asked to bring the process to some other area of their lives: to a school, a nursing home, a prison, a church, a cancer treatment program, a homeless shelter, a business or government agency. It might be where they work, where they play, or where they volunteer. It might be where their parents live or where their children go to school.

This enables group members to express their gratitude for a process that was given to them free of charge. It also helps the process extend free of charge to others who want to experience it. In this manner, the *Affinity Group Process* moves energetically into homes and organizations throughout the community, helping people learn to listen to one another and communicate in a non-threatening way. Wherever the process goes, healing happens, often in unexpected ways.

While the process is not outcome-oriented, wonderful results happen by themselves when people feel listened to and accepted. Because the process teaches us to accept others unconditionally and respect differences, it enables people from all different races, religions, social and economic groups to bond spiritually and come to a deeper appreciation and understanding of one another.

This simple spiritual practice can bring the presence of love and compassion to your relationship with your husband, your wife, or your children. It can bring understanding to your work environment, your neighborhoods, schools, hospitals, and prisons. It can bring people from different groups together in your city, your country, and ultimately the world that you live in. There are no limits to what it can do. And all because you have taken up the mantle. All because of your commitment to learn how to hold the space of unconditional love and acceptance for yourself and others. *

---

*The *Affinity Process* is described in detail in my book *Living in the Heart: The Affinity Process and the Path of Unconditional Love and Acceptance* (see order form in the back of this book). Affinity Groups are meeting all over the country and will soon be linked together by a newsletter, a yearly Affinities Retreat, and by trainings for facilitators.

Adam and Eve: The Return

When we learn how to forgive ourselves for our mistakes and how to hold what happens in our lives gently and compassionately, when we learn to care for, forgive, see the innocence of others and consider their happiness equally with our own, when we learn to practice acceptance, listening without judgment, and not-fixing with each person we meet, then we will find ourselves standing at the gates of the garden.

To enter the garden gates, we must give up selfishness, greed, struggle, sacrifice, shame, envy. The reign of fear and anger must end within our own minds. We cannot take these with us into the garden. Knowledge itself, which we fought for at such great price, must also fall away. To be in the garden, we must know in a very different way.

We must know not by thinking but by being and trusting. Problems dissolve when we tell the truth with compassion and listen without judgment. And our needs are met through our willingness to be flexible and cooperative. For, in the garden, there is plenty to go around. There is no reason to compete for resources.

People who try to enter the garden prematurely don't have the consciousness they need to sustain the garden experience. Without much ado, they find themselves standing outside the gates once again, wondering how they are going to make a living.

In the garden, we are continually challenged to live to our full potential, so "making a living" is not an issue. By living true to ourselves and expressing our talents joyfully, we automatically create the resources which are necessary for the fulfillment of our needs. As a result, we don't have to manipulate others or envy what they have. We bless people and feel grateful for their creative contributions. We celebrate their happiness. And they celebrate ours.

In the garden, exclusive or conditional love is not possible. Since love and compassion are the defining characteristics of the garden experience, no one can be excluded from them. Everyone in the garden loves and respects everyone else. Everyone wants only the best for each other person.

Garden inhabitants are anxious to share their love with everyone, even those on the other side of the gates. They are always inviting people to come in and visit. But for some reason, very few of the visitors stay. A single selfish or self-critical thought can catapult a visitor to the other side of the gates.

In the garden, worry or fear is almost unknown. When fear comes up, it is held so compassionately that it quickly dissolves, just as it did in the Affinity Group. In fact, it may be said that the garden is just like a big Affinity Group. Everyone follows the guidelines as a matter of course, yet you couldn't find a copy of them if you looked. There are no books in the garden. And the only concepts you will find seem to be written in people's hearts.

In times past, people called the garden "heaven." And that seemed fitting, since most people did not arrive there until well after they had left their physical bodies behind. But now that name seems a bit inaccurate, since people are arriving in the garden while remaining in their physical bodies.

The garden is one of the places Buber was talking about when he said that there are two worlds: the world of suffering and the world of grace. The world of suffering exists outside the gates. The world of grace exists inside them.

Whether we live inside or outside the gates depends on how we stand in relationship to one another. Do we stand as equals or as unequals? Is our intention to bless or to curse? Do we see one another as innocent or guilty?

In that sense, depending on the contents of our

consciousness, we are constantly moving back and forth between heaven and hell, the world of suffering and the world of grace. When we are in one world, only that world seems real to us, and the other one seems an illusion.

But the truth is that both worlds are real and both worlds are inside us. The garden is not a physical place, but a place within our minds. It is a state of consciousness.

When we know that the whole drama is happening in our own minds, we no longer need to look outside of ourselves for answers. Peace is here. And so is agitation. Not only that, but in peace there is room for agitation, and in agitation there is room for peace.

In our own minds, the two worlds come together. The flames of dawn meet the flames of dusk. Like earth, consciousness is turning, showing us its many sides: Its pathos and its overwhelming beauty.

Day and night appear so different, but dawn and dusk are one and the same. Right now, as colors flash at the horizon's edge, can you tell if day is surrendering to night, or night is surrendering to day?

When the vertical becomes horizontal, the divine is born in the human. Or perhaps the human is born in the divine. I wonder if it matters which.

Is Jesus God become man or man become God? Perhaps he is both...like the trickster God who lives between the two worlds.

I experience him as the embodiment of compassion, holding me in his loving embrace as I weep for the love I have lost and the errors I have made. And I also experience him ruthlessly cutting away my attachments and false beliefs. He is not one dimensional, but multi-dimensional: both soft and hard, gentle and fierce, reverent and irreverent.

In truth, I find that my teacher is as paradoxical as the lessons he teaches. He is hard to predict, hard to pin down. Whenever I think I'm doing well, he shakes his fist at me and warns me about being overconfident. And when I think I have really blown it, he puts his arm around me and assures me that all will be right.

What do I make of him? Well, he certainly isn't the pious, self-righteous teacher people have made him out to be. He is a perpetual troublemaker, a king of the jesters, a poet, a madman, and a revolutionary. He defies logic.

He represents the fullness of the human condition, with all its peculiarities and all its charm. He is authentic, honest, and real. All this I have come to know and appreciate.

May his words and understanding touch your heart as they have touched mine. May his love and compassion bring us all face to face in the garden of our innocence.

Namaste.

Paul Ferrini's unique blend of radical Christianity and other wisdom traditions, goes beyond self-help and recovery into the heart of healing. He is the author of twenty-one books including his latest books *I am the Door, Reflections of the Christ Mind* and *The Way of Peace.* His Christ Mind Series includes the bestseller *Love Without Conditions, The Silence of the Heart, Miracle of Love* and *Return to the Garden.* Other recent books include *Creating a Spiritual Relationship, Grace Unfolding, Living in the Heart, Crossing the Water, The Ecstatic Moment* and *Waking Up Together.*

Paul Ferrini is the founder and editor of *Miracles Magazine* and a nationally known teacher and workshop leader. His conferences, retreats, and Affinity Group Process have helped thousands of people deepen their practice of forgiveness and open their hearts to the divine presence in themselves and others. For more information on Paul's workshops and retreats or The Affinity Group Process, contact Heartways Press, P.O. Box 99, Greenfield, MA 01302-0099 or call 413-774-9474.

Books and Tapes
available from Heartways Press

I am the Door
by Paul Ferrini
ISBN 1-879159-41-4
288 pages hardcover
$21.95

Years ago, Paul Ferrini began hearing a persistent inner voice that said "I want you to acknowledge me." He also had a series of dreams in which Jesus appeared to teach him. Later, when Ferrini's relationship with his teacher was firmly established, the four books in the Reflections of the Christ Mind series were published. Here, in this lovely lyrical collection, we can hear the voice of Jesus speaking directly to us about practical topics of everyday life that our close to our hearts like work and livelihood, relationships, community, forgiveness, spiritual practices, and miracles.

When you put this book down, there will no doubt in your mind that the teachings of the master are alive today. Your life will never be the same.

The Way of Peace
A New System of Spiritual Guidance

Paul Ferrini

The Way of Peace
by Paul Ferrini
ISBN 1-879159-42-2
256 pages hardcover
$19.95

The Way of Peace is a simple method for connecting with the wisdom and truth that lie within our hearts. The two hundred and sixteen oracular messages in this book were culled from the bestselling *Reflections of the Christ Mind* series by Paul Ferrini.

Open this little book spontaneously to receive inspirational guidance, or ask a formal question and follow the simple divinatory procedure described in the introduction. You will be amazed at the depth and the accuracy of the response you receive.

Like the *I-Ching*, the *Book of Runes*, and other systems of guidance, *The Way of Peace* empowers you to connect with peace within and act in harmony with your true self and the unique circumstances of your life.

Special dice, blessed by the author, are available for using *The Way of Peace* as an oracle. To order these dice, send $3.00 plus shipping.

Our Surrender Invites Grace

Grace Unfolding:
The Art of Living A Surrendered Life
96 pages paperback $9.95
ISBN 1-879159-37-6

As we surrender to the truth of our being, we learn to relinquish the need to control our lives, figure things out, or predict the future.

We begin to let go of our judgments and interpretations and accept life the way it is. When we can be fully present with whatever life brings, we are guided to take the next step on our journey. That is the way that grace unfolds in our lives.

The Relationship Book You've Been Waiting For

Creating a Spiritual Relationship: A Guide to Growth and Happiness for Couples on the Path
144 pages paperback $10.95
ISBN 1-879159-39-2

This simple but profound guide to growth and happiness for couples will help you and your partner:

- Make a realistic commitment to each other
- Develop a shared experience that nurtures your relationship
- Give each other the space to grow and express yourselves as individuals
- Communicate by listening without judgment and telling the truth in a non-blaming way
- Understand how you mirror each other
- Stop blaming your partner and take responsibility for your thoughts, feelings and actions
- Practice forgiveness together on an ongoing basis

These seven spiritual principles will help you weather the ups and downs of your relationship so that you and your partner can grow together and deepen the intimacy between you. The book also includes a special section on living alone and preparing to be in relationship and a section on separating with love when a relationship needs to change form or come to completion.

175

Return to the Garden
Reflections of The Christ Mind,
Part IV
$12.95, Paperback
ISBN 1-879159-35-X

"In the Garden, all our needs were provided for. We knew no struggle or hardship. We were God's beloved. But happiness was not enough for us. We wanted the freedom to live our own lives. To
evolve, we had to learn to become love-givers, not just love-
receivers.

We all know what happened then. We were cast out of
the Garden and for the first time in our lives we felt shame,
jealousy, anger, lack. We experienced highs and lows, joy
and sorrow. Our lives became difficult. We had to work hard
to survive. We had to make mistakes and learn from them.

Initially, we tried to blame others for our mistakes. But
that did not make our lives any easier. It just deepened our
pain and misery. We had to learn to face our fears, instead
of projecting them onto each other.

Returning to the Garden, we are different than we were
when we left hellbent on expressing our creativity at any
cost. We return humble and sensitive to the needs of all. We
return not just as created, but as co-creator, not just as son
of man, but also as son of God."

Learn the Spiritual Practice
Associated with the Christ Mind Teachings

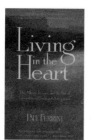

Living in the Heart The Affinity Process and the Path of Unconditional Love and Acceptance
Paperback $10.95
ISBN 1-879159-36-8

The long awaited, definitive book on the *Affinity Process* is finally here. For years, the *Affinity Process* has been refined by participants so that it could be easily understood and experienced. Now, you can learn how to hold a safe, loving, non-judgmental space for yourself and others which will enable you to open your heart and move through your fears. The *Affinity Process* will help you learn to take responsibility for your fears and judgments so that you won't project them onto others. It will help you learn to listen deeply and without judgment to others. And it will teach you how to tell your truth clearly without blaming others for your experience.

Part One contains an in-depth description of the principles on which the *Affinity Process* is based. Part Two contains a detailed discussion of the *Affinity Group Guidelines*. And Part Three contains a manual for people who wish to facilitate an *Affinity Group* in their community.

If you are a serious student of the *Christ Mind* teachings, this book is essential for you. It will enable you to begin a spiritual practice which will transform your life and the lives of others. It will also offer you a way of extending the teachings of love and forgiveness throughout your community.

Now Finally our Bestselling Title on Audio Tape

Love Without Conditions,
Reflections of the Christ Mind, Part I

by Paul Ferrini
The Book on Tape Read by the Author
2 Cassettes, Approximately 3.25 hours
ISBN 1-879159-24-4 $19.95
Now on audio tape: the incredible book
from Jesus calling us to awaken to our own Christhood.
Listen to this gentle, profound book while driving in your
car or before going to sleep at night. Elisabeth Kubler-
Ross calls this "the most important book I have read. I
study it like a Bible." Find out for yourself how this amazing book has helped thousands of people understand the
radical teachings of Jesus and begin to integrate these
teachings into their lives.

*With its heartfelt combination of sensuality
and spirituality, Paul Ferrini's poetry has been
compared to the poetry of Rumi.*

Crossing The Water:
Poems About Healing
and Forgiveness in
Our Relationships
The time for healing and reconciliation
has come, Ferrini writes. Our relationships
help us heal childhood wounds, walk
through our deepest fears, and cross over the water of
our emotional pain. Just as the rocks in the river are
pounded and caressed to rounded stone, the rough
edges of our personalities are worn smooth in the context of a committed relationship. If we can keep our

hearts open, we can heal together, experience genuine equality, and discover what it means to give and receive love without conditions.

With its heartfelt combination of sensuality and spirituality, Paul Ferrini's poetry has been compared to the poetry of Rumi. These luminous poems demonstrate why Paul Ferrini is first a poet, a lover and a mystic. Come to this feast of the beloved with an open heart and open ears. 96 pp. paper ISBN 1-879159-25-2 $9.95.

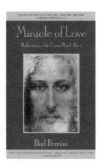

Miracle of Love: Reflections of the Christ Mind, Part III

In this volume of the Christ Mind series, Jesus sets the record straight regarding a number of events in his life. He tells us: "I was born to a simple woman in a barn. She was no more a virgin than your mother was." Moreover, the virgin birth was not the only myth surrounding his life and teaching. So were the concepts of vicarious atonement and physical resurrection.

Relentlessly, the master tears down the rigid dogma and hierarchical teachings that obscure his simple message of love and forgiveness. He encourages us to take him down from the pedestal and the cross and see him as an equal brother who found the way out of suffering by opening his heart totally. We too can open our hearts and find peace and happiness. "The power of love will make miracles in your life as wonderful as any attributed to me," he tells us. "Your birth into this embodiment is no less holy than mine. The love that you extend to others is no less important than the love I extend to you." 192 pp. paper ISBN 1-879159-23-6 $12.95.

Waking Up Together: Illuminations on the Road to Nowhere

There comes a time for all of us when the outer destinations no longer satisfy and we finally understand that the love and happiness we seek cannot be found outside of us. It must be found in our own hearts, on the other side of our pain. "The Road to Nowhere is the path through your heart. It is not a journey of escape. It is a journey through your pain to end the pain of separation."

This book makes it clear that we can no longer rely on outer teachers or teachings to find our spiritual identity. Nor can we find who we are in relationships where boundaries are blurred and one person makes decisions for another. If we want to be authentic, we can't allow anyone else to be an authority for us, nor can we allow ourselves to be an authority for another person.

Authentic relationships happen between equal partners who take responsibility for their own consciousness and experience. When their buttons are pushed, they are willing to look at the obstacles they have erected to the experience of love and acceptance. As they understand and surrender the false ideas and emotional reactions that create separation, genuine intimacy becomes possible, and the sacred dimension of the relationship is born. 216 pp. paper ISBN 1-879159-17-1 $14.95

The Ecstatic Moment: A Practical Manual for Opening Your Heart and Staying in It.

A simple, power-packed guide that helps us take appropriate responsibility for our experience and establish healthy boundaries with others. Part II contains many helpful exercises and meditations that teach us to stay centered, clear and open in heart and mind. The Affinity Group Process and other group practices help us learn important listening and communication skills that can transform our troubled relationships. Once you have read this book, you will keep it in your briefcase or on your bedside table, referring to it often. You will not find a more practical, down to earth guide to contemporary spirituality. You will want to order copies for all your friends. 128 pp. paper   ISBN 1-879159-18-X $10.95

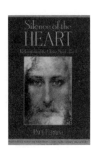

The Silence of the Heart: Reflections of the Christ Mind, Part II

A powerful sequel to *Love Without Conditions.* John Bradshaw says: "with deep insight and sparkling clarity, this book demonstrates that the roots of all abuse are to be found in our own self-betrayal. Paul Ferrini leads us skillfully and courageously beyond shame, blame, and attachment to our wounds into the depths of self-forgiveness…a must read for all people who are ready to take responsibility for their own healing." 218 pp. paper. ISBN 1-879159-16-3 $14.95

Love Without Conditions:
Reflections of the Christ Mind, Part I

An incredible book from Jesus calling us to awaken to our Christhood. Rarely has any book conveyed the teachings of the master in such a simple but profound manner. This book will help you to bring your understanding from the head to the heart so that you can model the teachings of love and forgiveness in your daily life. 192 pp. paper ISBN 1-879159-15-5 $12.00

The Wisdom of the Self

This ground-breaking book explores our authentic experience and our journey to wholeness. "Your life is your spiritual path. Don't be quick to abandon it for promises of bigger and better experiences. You are getting exactly the experiences you need to grow. If your growth seems too slow or uneventful for you, it is because you have not fully embraced the situations and relationships at hand...To know the Self is to allow everything, to embrace the totality of who we are, all that we think and feel, all of our fear, all of our love." 229 pp. paper ISBN 1-879159-14-7 $12.00

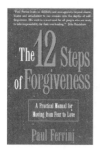

The Twelve Steps of Forgiveness

A practical manual for healing ourselves and our relationships. This book gives us a step-by-step process for moving through our fears, projections, judgments, and guilt so that we can take responsibility for creating the life we want. With great gentleness, we learn to embrace our lessons and to find equality with others. A must read for all in recovery and others seeking spiritual wholeness. 128 pp. paper ISBN 1-879159-10-4 $10.00

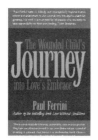

The Wounded Child's Journey: Into Love's Embrace

This book explores a healing process in which we confront our deep-seated guilt and fear, bringing love and forgiveness to the wounded child within. By surrendering our judgments of self and others, we overcome feelings of separation and dismantle co-dependent patterns that restrict our self-expression and ability to give and receive love. 225pp. paper ISBN 1-879159-06-6 $12.00

The Bridge to Reality

A Heart-Centered Approach to *A Course in Miracles* and the Process of Inner Healing. Sharing his experiences of spiritual awakening, Paul emphasizes self-acceptance and forgiveness as cornerstones of spiritual practice. Presented with beautiful photos, this book conveys the essence of *The Course* as it is lived in daily life. 192 pp. paper ISBN 1-879159-03-1 $12.00

Virtues of The Way

A lyrical work of contemporary scripture reminiscent of the *Tao Te Ching*. Beautifully illustrated, this inspirational book will help you cultivate the spiritual values required to fulfill your creative purpose and live in harmony with others. 64 pp. paper ISBN 1-879159-02-3 $7.50

From Ego to Self

108 illustrated affirmations designed to offer you a new way of viewing conflict situations so that you can overcome negative thinking and bring more energy, faith and optimism into your life. 144 pp. paper ISBN 1-879159-01-5 $10.00

The Body of Truth

A crystal clear introduction to the universal teachings of love and forgiveness. This book traces all forms of suffering to negative attitudes and false beliefs, which we have the ability to transform. 64 pp. paper ISBN 1-879159-02-3 $7.50

Available Light

Inspirational, passionate poems dealing with the work of inner integration, love and relationships, death and re-birth, loss and abundance, life purpose and the reality of spiritual vision. 128 pp. paper ISBN 1-879159-05-8 $12.00

Poetry and Guided Meditation Tapes
by Paul Ferrini

The Poetry of the Soul

With its heartfelt combination of sensuality and spirituality, Paul Ferrini's poetry has been compared to the poetry of Rumi. These luminous poems read by the author demonstrate why Paul Ferrini is first a poet, a lover and a mystic. Come to this feast of the beloved with an open heart and open ears. With Suzi Kesler on piano. $10.00 ISBN 1-879159-26-0

The Circle of Healing

The meditation and healing tape that many of you have been seeking. This gentle meditation opens the heart to love's presence and extends that love to all the beings in your experience. A powerful tape with inspirational piano accompaniment by Michael Gray. ISBN 1-879159-08-2 $10.00

Healing the Wounded Child

A potent healing tape that accesses old feelings of pain, fragmentation, self-judgment and separation and brings them into the light of conscious awareness and acceptance. Side two includes a hauntingly beautiful "inner child" reading from The Bridge to Reality with piano accompaniment by Michael Gray. ISBN 1-879159-11-2 $10.00

Forgiveness: Returning to the Original Blessing

A self healing tape that helps us accept and learn from the mistakes we have made in the past. By letting go of our judgments and ending our ego-based search for perfection, we can bring our darkness to the light, dissolving anger, guilt, and shame. Piano accompaniment by Michael Gray. ISBN 1-879159-12-0 $10.00

Paul Ferrini Talks and Workshop Tapes

Answering Our Own Call for Love

A Sermon given at the *Pacific Church of Religious Science* in San Diego, CA November, 1997

Paul tells the story of his own spiritual awakening: his Atheist upbringing, how he began to open to the presence of God, and his connection with Jesus and the Christ Mind teaching. In a very clear, heart-felt way, Paul presents to us the spiritual path of love, acceptance, and forgiveness. 1 Cassette $10.00 ISBN 1-879159-33-3

The Ecstatic Moment

A workshop given by Paul in Los Angeles at the *Agape International Center of Truth*, May, 1997

Shows us how we can be with our pain compassionately and learn to nurture the light within ourselves, even when it appears that we are walking through darkness. Discusses subjects such as living in the present, acceptance, not fixing self or others, being with our discomfort and learning that we are lovable as we are. 1 Cassette $10.00   ISBN 1-879159-27-9

Honoring Self and Other

A Workshop at the *Pacific Church of Religious Science* in San Diego, November, 1997

Helps us understand the importance of not betraying ourselves in our relationships with others. Focuses on understanding healthy boundaries, setting limits, and saying no to others in a loving way. Real life examples include a woman who is married to a man who is chronically critical of her, and a gay man who wants to tell his judgmental parents that he has AIDS. 1 Cassette $10.00   ISBN 1-879159-34-1

Seek First the Kingdom

Two Sunday Messages given by Paul: the first in May, 1997 in Los Angeles at the AGAPE INT'L. CENTER OF TRUTH, and the second in September, 1997 in Portland, OR at the *Unity Church*.

Discusses the words of Jesus in the Sermon on the Mount: "Seek first the kingdom and all else will be added to you." Helps us understand how we create the inner temple by learning to hold our judgments of self and other more compassionately. The love of God flows through our love and acceptance of ourselves. As we establish our connection to the divine within ourselves, we don't need to look outside of ourselves for love and acceptance. Includes fabulous music by The Agape Choir and Band. 1 Cassette $10.00   ISBN 1-879159-30-9

Double Cassette Tape Sets

Ending the Betrayal of the Self

A Workshop given by Paul at the *Learning Annex* in Toronto, April, 1997

A roadmap for integrating the opposing voices in our psyche so that we can experience our own wholeness. Delineates what our responsibility is and isn't in our relationships with others, and helps us learn to set clear, firm, but loving boundaries. Our relationships can become areas of sharing and fulfillment, rather than mutual invitations to co-dependency and self betrayal. 2 Cassettes $16.95 ISBN 1-879159-28-7

Relationships: Changing Past Patterns

A Talk with Questions and Answers Given at the *Redondo Beach Church of Religious Science,* November, 1997

Begins with a Christ Mind talk describing the link between learning to love and accept ourselves and learning to love and accept others. Helps us understand how we are invested in the past and continue to replay our old relationship stories. Helps us get clear on what we want and understand how to be faithful to it. By being totally committed to ourselves, we give birth to the beloved within and also without. Includes an in-depth discussion about meditation, awareness, hearing our inner voice, and the Affinity Group Process. 2 Cassettes $16.95 ISBN 1-879159-32-5

Relationship As a Spiritual Path

A workshop given by Paul in Los Angeles at the *Agape Int'l. Center of Truth*, May, 1997

Explores concrete ways in which we can develop a relationship with ourselves and learn to take responsibility for our own experience, instead of blaming others for our perceived unworthiness. Also discussed: accepting our differences, the new paradigm of relationship, the myth of the perfect partner, telling our truth, compassion vs. rescuing, the unavailable partner, abandonment issues, negotiating needs, when to say no, when to stay and work on a relationship and when to leave. 2 Cassettes $16.95 ISBN 1-879159-29-5

Opening to Christ Consciousness

A Talk with Questions & Answers at *Unity Church*, Tustin, CA November, 1997

Begins with a Christ Mind talk giving us a clear picture of how the divine spark dwells within each of us and how we can open up to God-consciousness on a regular basis. Deals with letting go and forgiveness in our relationships with our parents, our children and our partners. A joyful, funny, and scintillating tape you will want to listen to many times. 2 Cassettes $16.95 ISBN 1-879159-31-7

Risen Christ Posters and Notecards
11" x 17" Poster
suitable for framing
ISBN 1-879159-19-8 $10.00

Set of 8
Notecards
with Envelopes
ISBN   1-
879159-20-1
$10.00

Ecstatic Moment Posters and Notecards

8.5" x 11" Poster
suitable for framing
ISBN 1-879159-21-X $5.00

Set of 8
Notecards with
Envelopes
ISBN 1-879159-
22-8 $10.00

Heartways Press Order Form

Name _____

Address _____

City _____ State _____ Zip _____

Phone/Fax_____ Email _____

Books by Paul Ferrini

The Way of Peace Hardcover ($19.95)	_____
Way of Peace Dice ($3.00)	_____
I am the Door Hardcover ($21.95)	_____
Reflections of the Christ Mind: The Present Day	
Teachings of Jesus Hardcover (Available May, 2000)	_____
Creating a Spiritual Relationship ($10.95)	_____
Grace Unfolding: The Art of Living A	
Surrendered Life ($9.95)	_____
Return to the Garden ($12.95)	_____
Living in the Heart ($10.95)	_____
Miracle of Love ($12.95)	_____
Crossing the Water ($9.95)	_____
Waking Up Together ($14.95)	_____
The Ecstatic Moment ($10.95)	_____
The Silence of the Heart ($14.95)	_____
Love Without Conditions ($12.00)	_____
The Wisdom of the Self ($12.00)	_____
The Twelve Steps of Forgiveness ($10.00)	_____
The Circle of Atonement ($12.00)	_____
The Bridge to Reality ($12.00)	_____
From Ego to Self ($10.00)	_____
Virtues of the Way ($7.50)	_____
The Body of Truth ($7.50)	_____
Available Light ($10.00)	_____

Audio Tapes by Paul Ferrini

The Circle of Healing ($10.00) _____
Healing the Wounded Child ($10.00) _____
Forgiveness: The Original Blessing ($10.00) _____
The Poetry of the Soul ($10.00) _____
Seek First the Kingdom ($10.00) _____
Answering Our Own Call for Love ($10.00) _____
The Ecstatic Moment ($10.00) _____
Honoring Self and Other ($10.00) _____
Love Without Conditions ($19.95) 2 tapes _____
Ending the Betrayal of the Self ($16.95) 2 tapes _____
Relationships: Changing Past Patterns ($16.95) 2 tapes _____
Relationship As a Spiritual Path ($16.95) 2 tapes _____
Opening to Christ Consciousness ($16.95) 2 tapes _____

Posters and Notecards

Risen Christ Poster 11"x17" ($10.00) _____
Ecstatic Moment Poster 8.5"x11" ($5.00) _____
Risen Christ Notecards 8/pkg ($10.00) _____
Ecstatic Moment Notecards 8/pkg ($10.00) _____

Shipping

($2.50 for first item, $1.00 each additional item. _____
Add additional $1.00 for first class postage _____
and an extra $1.00 for hardcover books.) _____
MA residents please add 5% sales tax. _____
Please allow 1-2 weeks for delivery TOTAL _____

Send Order To: Heartways Press P. O. Box 99,
Greenfield, MA 01302-0099 413-774-9474
Toll free: 1-888-HARTWAY (Orders only)